THE vegan BRIDGE

THE vegan BRIDGE

EXPANDING
PLANT-BASED
CUISINE

whitecap

EDITOR Patrick Geraghty
PROOFREADER Patrick Geraghty
DESIGNER Andrew Bagatella
PHOTOGRAPHER Igor M. Aldomar
ADDITIONAL PHOTOGRAPHY FROM UNSPLASH Ehud Neuhaus (page 6), K8 (page 9), charlesdeluvio (page 12), Nathan Dumlao (page 15, 149), Kisoulou (page 18), Theme Photos (page 23)

Library and Archives Canada Cataloguing in Publication

Avril, Romain, author; Tablang, Richelle, author
The vegan bridge : adding plant-based flare to the carnivore's kitchen /
Romain Avril and Richelle Tablang.
Canadiana 20210120959 | ISBN 9781770503595 (softcover)
1. Vegan cooking. 2. Cookbooks.
LCC TX837 .A97 2021 | DDC 641.5/6362–dc23
Includes index.

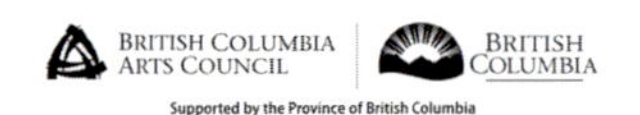

Whitecap Books acknowledges the financial support of the Government of Canada through the Canada Book Fund (CBF) for our publishing activities and the Province of British Columbia through the Book Publishing Tax Credit.

Printed in Hong Kong by Sheck Wah Tong Printing

"To our families, who've always taught us the importance and meaning of food, as well as its values."

TABLE OF CONTENTS

FOREWORD *by* Matthew Kenney

As a professional chef with a focus on shifting the global food paradigm towards plant-based for nearly 20 years, I am thrilled to recommend *The Vegan Bridge.* Given the world's long history of consuming animal products, as well as the foundations of how we learned to cook and eat, transitioning to a vegan diet can be a challenge without proper knowledge, tools and, of course, delicious recipes. This book provides all of these elements with dishes that are familiar and innovative and look absolutely delicious. I am grateful for creatives like Romain and Richelle who are working passionately to bring more plants to our dining tables and am so excited for everyone to experience this wonderful new book.

INTRODUCTION

In 2011, I served a high-end, 15-course vegan meal to a group with mixed dietary needs, determined not to leave anyone out. This was probably my first real experience catering a full plant-based meal while also being creative and not using the same ingredients twice. Utilizing different techniques, textures and cooking methods, it had to be original and beautiful to look at, while offering an exceptional experience to my vegan and omnivore guests alike. It was a true success and a lot of fun, and I have been serving innovative plant-based dishes at all of my restaurants ever since.

The two of us have served countless plates of vegan fare to guests with diverse dietary and culinary backgrounds. Whether it's a dinner for PETA or a birthday party for a self-aware young teen, we have routinely gone above and beyond. Richelle's desserts in particular always leave an impression—no small feat, as the technicality and science of pastry makes it way more difficult to achieve something exceptional using solely vegan ingredients.

A vegan cookbook written by two French-trained chefs who are also omnivores probably seems unorthodox. However, the world is changing, cuisine evolving, and we feel there is an important need to build a bridge between the vegan and omnivore realms. Both of us have always believed that our primary job as food professionals is to elevate, satiate and innovate, and in this book we are here to creatively bridge the divide, using our fine-dining experience to present a full range of ideas from the most practical and everyday vegan staples to sophisticated recipes that showcase the incredible potential of plant-based foods. Incorporating a few vegan meals into everyday life can be done simply and without sacrificing flavour or presentation, and our recipes will keep your meals exciting no matter which side of the bridge you typically land on.

More than a casual collection of simplistic well-worn recipes that masquerade vegetables as meat or find substitutes, this book aims to highlight the nutritious and flavourful possibilities of vegan cooking without compromise. We pack our recipes with texture and flavour while maintaining approachability, visual beauty and nutritional integrity. We are not here to convert the world to an all-vegan diet. Our goal is purely to illustrate the benefits of sprinkling vegan flair into your meals, with recipes that are equally as enticing as any meat dish.

We also want to impress the importance of sustainability and seasonality, as it is essential to eat produce when it's meant to be harvested. Yes, nowadays you can enjoy strawberries or tomatoes all year long, but at what price? Flavours and nutrients will definitely lose out. Just as it wouldn't be fair to judge someone on a bad day, produce should be judged at its peak—when it's full of sun and grown the way the earth intended.

Pay attention to what goes into your body, and consider where it has come from. Is it local, sustainable, in season? Do I know the farmer? Is it good for me? Should I be eating it right now? These are all questions we should be asking ourselves. Remember that food is healing, but only if consumed properly. We must respect our alimentation.

Of course, we don't mean to suggest you cannot enjoy a plum or a peach in the middle of winter. What matters is that your produce was harvested in its prime and properly preserved. Pickled, canned, frozen, cured—these are a few techniques among many that will allow you to eat well and enjoy your favourite foods all year long. And truly, there are few better feelings than biting into summer in the middle of winter when the afternoons are dark, and the cold weather freezes our bones.

—Romain

BUILDING A VEGAN BRIDGE

ROMAIN: Along the path to an omnivorous lifestyle, my cooking was the first thing to adapt, followed by my diet. I began to find that promoting the use of sustainable meat wasn't enough—I had to put more of an effort into the way I eat. This is where I bridged into a new diet.

At first I found some pushback both from within the restaurant industry and from the general public—a perception that you had to be either/or. But I don't like labels, and I truly believe people should be able to tap into any diet they choose, so long as they're health conscious. So enough was enough. I decided to use my voice and creativity for everyone in search of a safe place to cook and to enjoy vegan food without being hampered by labelling. And with that, *The Vegan Bridge* was born.

RICHELLE: I am not vegan. I love meat, and I love cheese. I do, however, understand the benefits of plant-based eating both for dietary and ethical reasons. My respect and appreciation for a well-crafted vegan meal is extraordinary, and in this sense I think Romain and I come from a powerful perspective as carnivores talking about vegan food. I've gone my entire life with meat included in at least one meal of every day, but the dishes in this book are so flavourful and fun that the idea of using them to replace a meat-based meal every so often doesn't feel like a chore, or as if the absence of animal proteins comes at a cost. Our attempt here is to create a connection between other non-vegans, just like us, and have them delve into the world of veganism without having to commit completely to a meat-free life. The easiest way in which we see ourselves doing this is by creating dishes that we would normally create in the places we work—places where people expect a certain pedigree of execution and skill. We set out to create dishes that people would be excited to try whether they're vegan or not, and to provide already-committed vegans with ideas on how to elevate their skills and cooking comfort to a new level. We're creating a bridge from our professional training to your home cooking, from non-vegans to vegans.

PANTRY ESSENTIALS

Here you will find the ingredients that are the most essential to making the recipes in this cookbook. Although they can be substituted, we highly encourage you to stock up so you don't find yourself stranded and unable to accomplish your best work in the kitchen.

AGAR-AGAR: A gelling agent made from seaweed. Typically available in health food stores or Asian supermarkets, it is used in a powdered form. Agar activates at 85–90°C (185–195°F) and sets at 35–40°C (95–105°F).

ALMOND MILK: Used to replace dairy milk, it can be found in a grocery store's non-dairy milk section either refrigerated or non-refrigerated. Keeps well in the fridge after being opened.

AQUAFABA: The liquid in a can of chickpeas that can be used as an egg white replacer. Keeps in the fridge for a week. To increase its strength, heat on low for about 30 minutes until half the liquid evaporates.

BEANS: A very good source of protein with many uses. Keep dried beans in a sealed bag and store in a dry storage area.

BLACK PEPPER: A great partner to kosher salt, it is best when added to a mill and cracked fresh (a better alternative to ground black pepper). Keeps for about 1 month before losing its flavour.

COCOA BUTTER: Fat derived from cocoa beans. It is incorporated into recipes to produce a rich, velvety texture.

COCONUT CREAM: Usually found in cans. Store in a dry place, then refrigerate once opened. Use as a replacement for heavy cream.

COCONUT MILK: A replacement for dairy milk that can be found refrigerated or non-refrigerated in the non-dairy milk section of a grocery store. Keeps well in the fridge after being opened.

COCONUT OIL: Great for cooking, it keeps well when sealed and should be placed in a dry storage area. It has a high smoke point, which means you can use it to cook things at a high heat. Keep in mind this oil is really fragrant. It can also be used as a spread in place of butter.

DRIED FRUITS: A great source of antioxidants and fibres, they are great to add to a recipe or eat on their own as a snack. Keep in a sealed bag in a dry storage area.

EGG REPLACER: Found in the baking section near the flours, this does exactly what its name indicates. It is high in protein, and with high cholesterol and no saturated fat it can be healthier than eggs. Keep sealed in its original package and place in a dry storage area.

GRAINS: Another huge source or proteins and fibres. Can be bought dry or in cans. If dry, grains must be soaked and cooked with vegetable stock and aromatics before use.

KOSHER SALT: A gentler salt than table salt in terms of flavour, but with a coarser grain. Keep in a sealed container in a dry storage area.

MALT POWDER: A powder made from pulverized barley and wheat flour. Can be used to enhance the flavour and texture of bread and add a depth to the browning and crust.

MALT SYRUP: A natural sweetener extracted from malted barley. Can be used to add complexity to the flavour profile of bread and help colour the dough without overbaking.

MAPLE SYRUP: A great natural sugar. The clearer, the better. It is a much better sweetener than refined sugar.

MISO: Fermented soybean paste that is great emulsified, and can be used to add umami to dishes. It keeps really well in the fridge, tightly sealed.

NUTRITIONAL YEAST: Found in specialty stores, it has a strong umami flavour. Typically used to replace cheese in recipes, it also offers lots of nutrients. Keep sealed in a dry storage area.

NUTS: A great source of many nutrients and antioxidants, nuts are ideal for adding flavour and texture to a dish. They will keep for a while when sealed and placed in a dry storage area; however, they will lose their freshness after a couple weeks.

OAT MILK: A common replacement for dairy milk that can be found refrigerated or non-refrigerated in the non-dairy milk section of a grocery store. Keeps well in the fridge after being opened.

PECTIN: Used as a gelling agent, it is usually combined with sugar and acid to produce fruit-based items such as jam. In this book it used in a powdered form, although it is also available in a liquid form and can be purchased organically from the fruits it naturally occurs in.

SOY: Made from fermented soybeans, it has a great umami flavour. Perfect for dressings and sauces and used in the preparation of various dishes. Keeps well in the fridge after it has been opened. Tamari is the gluten-free alternative.

SOY MILK: A replacement for dairy milk that can be found refrigerated or non-refrigerated in the non-dairy milk section of a grocery store. Keeps well in the fridge after being opened.

SPICES: Heavily used in many cultures, they add a lot of flavour when mixed into a dish. Keep tightly sealed in a dry storage area.

TAHINI: Made from sesame, this paste keeps well after it's been opened if sealed in the fridge. It's great for emulsifying and has a pungent flavour.

TEMPEH: A great source of protein made from soybeans, it is considered healthier than tofu. Can be found fresh or dried.

TOFU: Bean curd that can be found refrigerated in a grocery store. It's a great protein and ideal main component in a meal, and keeps for a week or so when sealed and stored in the fridge.

VEGAN BUTTER (OR NON-HYDROGENATED STICK MARGARINE): A vegan alternative to regular butter that should be sealed and stored in fridge.

VEGETABLE OIL: Great for cooking as well as using in dressings, it keeps well when sealed and placed in a dry storage area. Its high smoke point means you can use it to cook things at a high temperature.

VEGETABLE STOCK: Can be made fresh or purchased from a store. Keeps well when sealed in the fridge, and can be used to cook beans and grains, or to make soups and stews.

XANTHAN GUM: A powdered product used to help thicken, stabilize and emulsify mixtures.

A NOTE ABOUT PRODUCE

For most of the recipes in this book, you'll need to keep well stocked with fresh produce. Whatever the source of your fruits, herbs and vegetables, washing them properly is essential and should be carried out before attempting any recipe. Wash your produce thoroughly under cold water and pat dry with a clean towel.

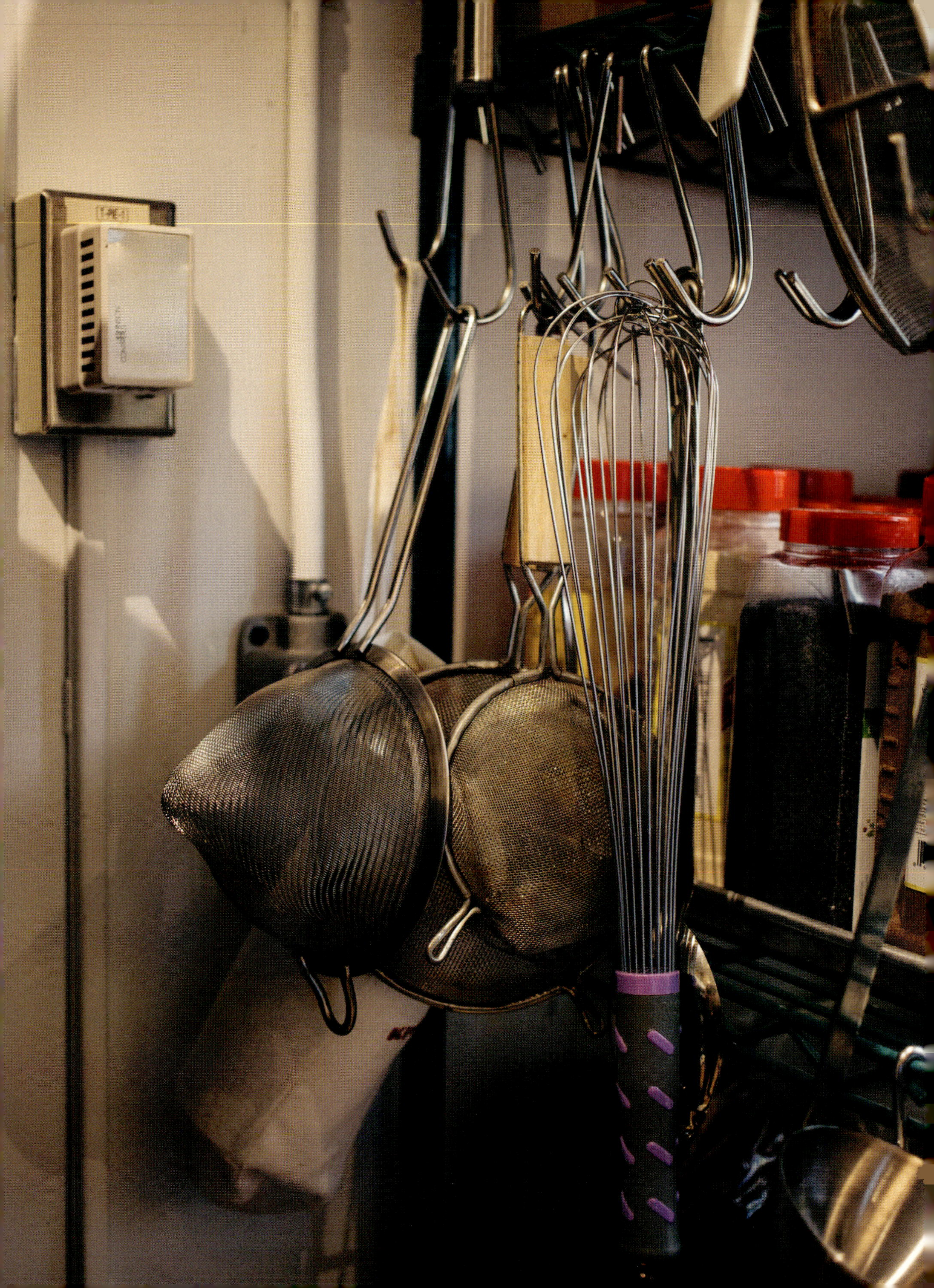

EQUIPMENT

There seems to be a tool for everything these days. Let us help you navigate! This is our list of equipment that not every kitchen will have, but that we recommend you consider in order to make our recipes as easy and manageable as possible. Items with a star next to them are the ones we think are most necessary to help set yourself up for success!

*BAKING SHEETS: Flat, sturdy baking sheets are the key to evenly cooked and roasted recipes, as well as even-layered cakes and doughs.

BUNDT OR CHIFFON PAN: The easiest way to make a basic, boring cake look more appealing is to bake it in a pretty, embellished mold! It also makes portioning a breeze.

CAST IRON SKILLET: Durable and able to withstand high temperatures, these have impeccable heat retention. They sear, fry, braise and bake! Make sure you're seasoning and caring for these precious babies.

CHEESECLOTH: Loosely woven cloth primarily used for—you guessed it—cheese production! However, it also makes the perfect thin barrier for straining liquids and separating even the tiniest solid particles.

CHINOIS: Cone-shaped strainers made of metal and fine mesh. Helpful for achieving smoother consistencies of stocks, soups, sauces, purées and more.

CIRCULATOR/SOUS-VIDE MACHINE: Not exclusive to the pros anymore! Best utilized for precise temperature control with consistent results. Great for slow cooking at low temperatures and infusing ingredients without losing any flavours.

*COOLING RACK/RESTING RACK/WIRE RACK: Cooling racks are necessary if you want to cool down hot items quickly and evenly. Leaving an item to cool on the hot vessel it was cooked in risks further cooking from residual heat, or excess moisture from condensation. No one wants a soggy bottom! You can also cook on a rack for even air circulation, roast or broil on it or use it to assist in dusting/glazing pastries.

DEHYDRATOR: A food dehydrator does exactly what it claims—it dehydrates your food. That is, it preserves your food by drying it out and reducing the moisture content, thereby preventing certain bacteria from growing and spoiling the item. We use it to help change up the textures of some of our favourite ingredients.

***FOOD PROCESSOR:** Used to blend, chop, dice and blitz. This instrument saves you a lot of time in repetitive or labour-intensive tasks. It's similar to a blender, but unlike a blender can handle items with minimal liquid.

HAND MIXER: We love our stand mixer, but sometimes a handheld mixer just does the trick. Best used with smaller quantities of items, or non-fussy items that need a quick whipping.

***HIGH-SPEED BLENDER:** A great time-saving tool for mixing, puréeing, blending, chopping and emulsifying. Sauces, smoothies, soups and salad dressings have never been smoother—or easier!

IMMERSION BLENDER: Lightweight and easy to use, especially with smaller-quantity items that just need a quick blitz! Also known as a hand or stick blender.

KITCHEN SCALE: Inexpensive and a saviour in the kitchen that helps make recipes exceptionally accurate and precise. We converted all our recipes into the metric system for you to easily scale everything out, but we still recommend every kitchen have one!

MANDOLINE: A cutting instrument with an adjustable blade that lets you slice as thin or thick as you'd like, with different blade attachments to give you different cuts! Since investing in a meat slicer is probably off the table, owning a mandoline will do the trick for recipes that require super thin slices.

MICROPLANE: There is nothing micro about the job this tool does. It's the easiest way to grate, mince and zest. Also known as a rasp.

NONSTICK BAKING MAT: Made of fibreglass and silicone and able to withstand extreme heats, nonstick mats make cooking and baking 100 times easier, with effortless clean up. Silpat is the ideal brand to seek out, as generic brands of a lesser quality may not do the job.

OFFSET SPATULA: Set yourself up for success by purchasing an offset spatula. They come in different sizes and are perfect for evenly spreading batters and frostings. You can also use them while cooking to help flip small or delicate items in a pan, or to lift hot items off a tray.

***PARCHMENT PAPER:** An excellent way to keep your counters and prep station clean and organized, parchment paper is typically used to line baking trays. Nonstick sheets save the day!

PASTA SHEETER: Used to get super thin and even sheets of pasta dough. Simple and fun to use, you'll want to make homemade pasta every night.

PIPING TIPS: Here's a tip—invest in a small army of piping tips! If you love to bake and decorate, tips are super useful when evenly decorating or piping intricate shapes. The ones we use in this book include various sizes of plain round tips, star tips, French star tips and the St. Honoré tip.

***PLASTIC FOOD WRAP:** Keep things fresh and moisture-locked with cling film.

***ROLLING PIN:** Stop getting flour all over your wine bottles as you try to MacGyver a rolling pin from spare parts. A classic rolling pin is the best way to roll out your dough as flat and evenly as possible.

ROUND CAKE PANS: Having multiple pans of the same size saves you time when baking multilayered cakes. Our recipes are tailored for 8- and 9-inch (20 and 23 cm) round cake pans.

SAUTEUSE: Put that Le Creuset casserole dish from your wedding registry to use! Particularly great for sautéing and braising, any heavy duty, deep-lipped sauté pan with a lid will do.

SILICONE MOLDS: Think of the aforementioned nonstick baking mats, but in different shapes and sizes. Now think of the endless possibilities!

SIPHON AND N2O CHARGERS: You know that metal canister they use at your favourite coffee shop to spray whipped cream all over the drinks? Get one. Nitrous oxide chargers are sold separately.

STAND MIXER: If you love to be in the kitchen, this is one of the greatest investments you can shell out for. Sure, it will whip, paddle and form any dough you throw in there, but separate attachments open up a new world of creative possibilities—from pasta to ice cream and beyond!

TAMIS: A wide, round, flat drum sieve. Perfect for sifting flour and dry ingredients. Also perfect for thicker purées when you need a large surface area to easily push it through. However, any old sifter will do!

TART RINGS: Essential for making perfectly round and individually sized tarts. In a pinch you can use a muffin tin, but it won't be quite the same.

***THERMOMETER:** Sometimes we can't eyeball things, and when precision is essential, cooking thermometers are here to save the day.

VACUUM SEALER: Some of our recipes require airtight seals on food in order to compress and infuse ingredients, or to drop into a sous vide–prepared tub. These sealers also come in handy for storage and leftovers!

CULINARY TERMS *and* TECHNIQUES

The kitchen can be an intimidating enough place without a bunch of inscrutable lingo that might scare you away from the best place in the house. Below we have put together a selection of frequently used terms that are common to the book and life as a chef. Don't worry, we've got your back.

BAIN-MARIE: Also known as a double boiler. A cooking vessel in which ingredients are placed in a bowl on top of a low-simmering pot of water. The ingredients are not in direct contact with the heat source and can gently cook or melt.

BATTER: A mixture, usually with a base of flour and liquid, that is thin enough to be spooned or poured (such as pancake, cake or frying batter).

BATONS: An item cut into medium rectangles (like matchsticks) that are roughly 2–3 inches (5–7 cm) long and ¼–½ inch (0.5–1 cm) thick.

BLANCHING: Process in which items are cooked in boiling water for a brief amount of time, then quickly transferred to ice water in order to shock and halt the cooking.

BLITZING: Puréeing or mixing ingredients at quick intervals with high power. Usually refers to the use of a high-speed blender, food processor or hand mixer.

BRAISING: Cooking method in which food is first seared at a high temperature in oil/fat, then slowly cooked at a lower heat with added liquid. This maintains the natural juices and flavours while also tenderizing.

BREADING: Coating an item (with flour, breadcrumbs, etc.) before cooking to create a crisp texture and help seal in moisture.

BRUNOISE: To cut an item into ⅛-inch (3 mm) cubes with a knife.

BULK FERMENTATION: The first period of rest when preparing a leavened dough, and the first stage of proofing. This resting time allows the yeast to activate and interact with the carbohydrates, expelling carbon dioxide and permitting the dough to expand and rise.

CARAMELIZING: Cooking process in which heated sugar begins to brown, releasing sweet and nutty flavour profiles.

CHIFFONADE: A knife cut used for leafy items in which the leaves are stacked and rolled up together before being sliced thin. The end result is long strips or thin ribbons.

CHOPPING: The process of cutting food items into pieces that are rough and less refined than with other knife cuts. Also refers to the cooking competition show *Chopped Canada* in which our own Chef Romain Avril once competed (in Season 3, Episode 24: Cooking for Love)!

CHOUX PASTRY DOUGH (OR PÂTE À CHOUX): What the French refer to as piping dough, used for items such as profiteroles, éclairs, gougères and more! The original round piped cream puffs resembled cabbages ("choux" in French), which inspired the name. Leavening in the dough is primarily from the moisture in the batter, which steams and expands during baking.

COMPOTE: A French cooking term that refers to a mixture of fruits cooked in sugar and aromatics. The fruit in compote is usually cooked in whole pieces or chunks and retains some structure after cooking.

CONFIT: A process of "preserving" an item that typically refers to slow-cooking over low heat for a period of time in oil/fat (for meats and vegetables) or sugar syrup (for fruits).

COUCHE: A cloth made of heavy duty French linen that is used in the final proofing stage of a bread. The canvas helps hold the final shape of the dough and dries out any excess moisture for a crispier crust.

COUVERTURE CHOCOLATE: High-quality chocolate with a high percentage of cocoa butter, which creates better flavour, texture, snap and shine. Used in tempering chocolate.

CRAQUELIN: Thin-rolled sugar dough that is cut into shapes and placed atop choux pastry before baking to form a crispy, sweet crust.

CRUMB: The interior texture and structure of baked bread.

CUTTING IN: To "cut in" butter or shortening is to incorporate the fats into the flour of a dough so that little clumps of butter remain whole in the mix. This is usually done with a pastry cutter, blender or fork and cold fats, and is the key to creating a flaky dough.

DEEP FRYING: Cooking process in which an item is cooked by completely submerging it in hot fat or oil.

DEGASSING: The process of "punching" down a dough, usually after bulk fermentation. This releases any excess gas bubbles and evens out the rise of the dough, making sure it has a properly formed and even crumb.

DEGLAZING: The process of adding liquid to a pan after cooking/searing an item. Loosens any food particles from the bottom of the pan and incorporates them back into the liquid, boosting the flavour profile.

DESEEDING: To remove all the seeds from an item.

DICING: Cutting an item into even-sided cubes with a knife. A large dice is about ¾ inch (2 cm), a medium dice is about ½ inch (6 mm) and a small dice is about ¼ inch (5 mm).

DOCKING: Pricking a pastry dough before baking in order to allow steam to escape, thereby promoting even baking without excess puffing. This can be achieved using a fork or with a special docking tool.

DOUBLE BOILER: See *bain-marie.*

DOUGH: A mixture, usually with a base of flour and liquid, that is thick and stiff and thus able to be kneaded or rolled.

DRIZZLING: The process of pouring a liquid in a fine stream to decorate or distribute evenly over a surface.

DUSTING: The process of sprinkling a powdered substance (like icing sugar or flour) evenly onto a surface, usually by passing it through a fine sifter to remove any clumps.

EGG REPLACER: A manufactured egg substitute, usually powdered, that is sold at health food stores or in the organic section of a grocery store.

EGG WASH: Liquid brushed over a pastry that is used to seal dough, or that is applied before baking to create a shine and even out browning. Traditionally made of eggs but revised into a vegan alternative for this book!

EMULSIFYING: The process of smoothly and thoroughly combining liquids that do not easily come together, like oil and water.

FINAL PROOF: The final stage of fermentation when making leavened doughs that occurs after shaping and dividing the dough, right before baking. An item is ready to bake when a gentle touch of the dough springs back slowly and leaves a small indent. If the dough springs back quickly, it needs to proof longer.

FLATTOP: Also known as a plancha, a flattop grill is a large, flat cooking surface. You can cook directly on the grill itself or cook overtop in pots and pans just like a regular range/stove. They are especially great for searing, toasting and frying.

FLORETS: Small, tight clusters of buds, usually in reference to bite-sized pieces of broccoli or cauliflower.

FOLD: When preparing a leavened dough, a basic fold is when you stretch and pull the dough then "fold" it back onto itself (usually in a round ball or loose rectangle). This releases excess gasses formed by the yeast, strengthens the gluten formation and equalizes the temperature of the dough.

FOLDING (DOUBLE): In laminated doughs, this is when the dough is folded like a book. We offset the initial fold to one side to ensure a more even lamination.

FOLDING (SINGLE): In laminated doughs, this is when the dough is folded like a letter into three equal parts.

FORTIFIED STOCK: Also known as double stock, this is a stock that has been cooked twice and therefore is richer and more concentrated in flavour. Can be made from normal stock by cooking down until reduced by half.

FRANGIPANE: A velvety, almond pastry filling typically made of butter, sugar, eggs and ground almonds.

GANACHE: A thick glaze or filling traditionally made of chocolate and cream.

GARNISH: Something used to decorate and embellish a dish, usually an edible item that compliments or reinforces the flavours of the dish while adding colour, texture and visual appeal.

GELÉE: A jellied food produced by stabilizing liquid with gelatin or a gelling agent.

GLUCOSE: A liquid sugar substance used to sweeten, thicken and soften a texture by preserving moisture.

GRANITÉ: Frozen dessert typically consisting of water, sugar and fruit juice that is frozen as a block and scraped at with a fork to form coarse ice crystals.

GREASING: The process of using oil or fat to coat a pan and prevent food from sticking to it.

INFUSING: Extracting and incorporating flavours from one item into another.

ISOMALT: A sugar substitute that does not caramelize like normal sugar, creating a clearer product that can be used for sugar candy creations, decorations and sculptures.

JOCONDE: A type of sponge cake. Light and airy and made with almond flour, it is mostly used in layered French cakes.

JULIENNE: To cut an item into thin rectangles similar to batons but smaller and finer.

KNEADING: The process of mixing a dough with your hands to encourage gluten formation.

LAMINATED DOUGH: The type of dough used in puff pastry and viennoiseries (croissants, danishes, etc.). Layers of butter and dough are created by making a series of folds in the dough that result in flaky, airy layers.

LOCK IN: When preparing laminated doughs, this is the step in which a pad of butter (beurrage) is encased within the pad of dough (détrempe). This "locks" the fat in the dough so that it can be rolled out and folded.

MARINADE: A mixture in which items are soaked for a duration of time so that they can absorb flavours and tenderize.

MEDALLION: A puck-shaped portion of food.

MESH STRAINER: A basic metal tool used to filter suspended solids from liquids. Also known as a sieve.

MINCING: The process of dicing food very finely.

MIREPOIX: A basic combination from classic French cooking that slowly sautées onions, celery and carrots as the base aromatics for soups, stocks, sauces and more.

PAIN D'ÉPICES: A French spiced cake (gingerbread loaf) classically made with rye, honey and spices.

PASS: To "pass" something means to strain or sift through a tamis, sieve or mesh strainer. This gets rid of any unwanted lumps and helps create smoother textures.

PEAKS: The shapes formed by whipping a substance such as meringue or cream to determine its level of stabilization. Soft peaks have little structure and a droopy consistency when spooned, while medium peaks have a little more hold and stiff/hard peaks have the firmest structure and shape.

PICKING: To "pick" something (i.e., herbs) is the process of plucking the leaves from the stems.

PICKLING: The process of brining and preserving items through anaerobic fermentation. Usually achieved with vinegar.

PIPING: Squeezing a mixture through the tip of a pastry bag while decorating to create a clean shape. Different tips are used for different shapes and outcomes.

POACHING: Cooking process in which an item is submerged in hot liquid to gently cook it while preserving its structural integrity.

PRICKING: The process of punching tiny holes into an item, usually with a fork or knife, to help it cook evenly.

PROOFING: While preparing bread, this is the period of resting during which fermentation occurs and the yeast leavens the dough.

PURÉE: A smooth, creamy liquid obtained through blending (puréeing).

RESERVE: To set something aside for future use.

ROUND UP: Refers to the process of forming a leavened dough into a smooth ball before resting/bulk fermentation. This is achieved by tightly folding the ends of the dough into the centre and flipping the dough over into a bowl so that the smooth, round bottom is now on top.

ROUX: Flour and fat that are cooked together on a stove. This mixture is used in classic French cooking as a base to thicken sauces, soups, stews and so on.

SACHET: Herbs, spices and aromatics that are tied together inside a pouch made of cheesecloth. This is added while cooking to make it easier to remove all the spices at once.

SCORING: Cutting clean slits into the surface of an item using a sharp knife or blade. This method can help in tenderizing, flavour absorption, even-cooking, maintaining the shape of an item or allowing excess steam to escape.

SCRAPING: Removing the skin of an item (e.g., ginger) by running a utensil over it to lift the skin away. When referring to a vanilla bean, this is the process of splitting the bean in half lengthwise with a sharp paring knife. The beans inside are then gently scraped out of the pod and reserved.

SEARING: Cooking at high heat to form a quick, caramelized brown crust.

SEASONING: To adjust the taste of an item to the liking of your palate.

SEGMENTING: The technique used to remove all the white pith from citrus fruits. The segments are the leftover slices of fruit.

SHALLOW FRYING: The cooking process in which an item is cooked in a small amount of hot fat/oil, as opposed to deep frying.

SHOCKING: The process of introducing a hot item to a cold environment in order to halt the cooking process. This can be done by submerging a hot item into ice cold water, running it under cold water or placing it in a blast freezer.

SIEVE: See *mesh strainer.*

SIMMERING: Cooking just below the boiling point.

SLIVERS: Thin, narrow cuts.

SMASHING: To use your hand or the side of a knife to crush an item, releasing the aroma and flavour.

SMOKE POINT: The temperature at which oil/fat begins to burn and smoke.

SOUS-VIDE COOKING: A cooking process that uses a food circulator. Food is vacuum sealed and submerged in a temperature-regulated water bath to cook at a lower temperature for a longer amount of time.

SPRINKLING: To evenly scatter something over the surface of an item.

STEEPING: Extracting and incorporating flavours from an item into a liquid by heating them together.

STRAINING: Separating the solids and liquids in a mixture by passing them through a perforated utensil.

SWEATING: A cooking process in which items are gently cooked in oil/fat until soft, releasing their moisture and aromatics.

TAPIOCA MALTODEXTRIN: A powdered substance derived from tapioca starch that is used in molecular gastronomy to play with texture and thicken liquid fats.

TEMPERING (CHOCOLATE): The process of heating and cooling high-quality chocolate to specific temperatures in order to properly stabilize the crystals inside. The tempered chocolate is used as a coating, shell or dip for candies or bonbons, as well as to make chocolate decorations. Properly tempered chocolate will have a crisp snap when bit into and a glossy shine, and it won't melt as easily when touched.

TOASTED NUTS AND SEEDS: Nuts and seeds that have been roasted in the oven or toasted on a dry skillet until golden brown. If toasting them yourself, it's good to keep the heat medium to low to avoid burning.

WEDGES: Triangular pieces typically cut from round/oval items such as apples, lemons or potatoes. They are wider at the edge and taper towards the centre.

YEAST (DRY INSTANT): A natural, single-celled organism used in fermentation. In this book, yeast is typically used in a dry, instant form to help leaven dough, but it is also available in an active dry form, a rapid/quick-rise form and a fresh form.

DIPS *and* SPREADS

ROASTED RED PEPPER HUMMUS

BABA GANOUSH

SPINACH DIP

MAKES ABOUT 2 CUPS (500 ML)

- 2 Tbsp (30 mL) grapeseed oil
- 2 cloves garlic, minced
- ½ onion, finely brunoised
- 1¼ lb (560 g) spinach leaves
- 1 Tbsp (15 mL) rice flour
- ½ lb (225 g) vegan cream cheese
- 2 Tbsp (30 mL) nutritional yeast
- ¼ cup (60 mL) soy milk (or other non-dairy milk)
- ¼ tsp (1 mL) kosher salt
- ⅛ tsp (0.5 mL) fresh black pepper

Who doesn't love a good spinach dip? This creamy and garlicky dip will be best enjoyed with bread or even crunchy vegetables. Serve alongside the Artichoke Dip (see below) as part of a Crudité Platter (page 54).

In a medium skillet, heat the grapeseed oil over medium-high heat. Add the garlic and onion and cook until golden brown, stirring occasionally. Add the spinach leaves and cook until soft.

Remove the spinach from the pan and let it cool, then squeeze all the water out. Return the spinach to the skillet, stir in the flour and cook for another 1–2 minutes over medium-low heat. Add the vegan cream cheese and cook until melted, then add the yeast and non-dairy milk; cook for 2 more minutes. Season with salt and pepper.

Best enjoyed hot, but you can also serve it at room temperature. Store in a sealed airtight container up to 3 days in the fridge.

ARTICHOKE DIP

MAKES ABOUT 3 CUPS (750 ML)

- 1 Tbsp (15 mL) olive oil
- ½ onion, diced
- 3 cloves garlic, minced
- ½ cup (125 mL) vegetable stock (for homemade, see page 114)
- 2 cups (500 mL) canned artichoke hearts
- ½ cup (125 mL) raw unsalted cashews, soaked overnight and drained
- 1 Tbsp (15 mL) lemon juice
- 1 Tbsp (15 mL) nutritional yeast
- 4 stalks thyme, leaves picked and chopped
- 1 tsp (5 mL) truffle paste
- 1 pinch chili flakes
- ½ tsp (2 mL) sea salt
- 8 stalks flat parsley, finely chopped

Just like mine, an artichoke's heart can be hard to find, but once you peel back the layers you end up with a soft and sweet nugget of gold. Although you can use fresh artichoke hearts when in season, you'll find them in cans all year long. The addition of truffle paste to this dip is unique and will please your guests. Serve as part of a well-arranged Crudité Platter (page 54) along with the Spinach Dip (see above).

In a medium skillet, heat the olive oil over medium heat; add the onion and garlic and sweat until the onion becomes translucent. Remove pan from heat and cool slightly.

Add the cooked onion mixture to a high-speed blender with the canned artichokes, cashews, lemon juice, nutritional yeast, thyme, truffle paste, chili flakes and salt. Blend until smooth. Fold in the chopped parsley and transfer the mixture to a small bowl to serve.

BABA GANOUSH

MAKES ABOUT 2 CUPS (500 ML)

I have always been a big fan of spices and flavours from the Middle East. Served with Roasted Red Pepper Hummus (page 37) and Pita Bread (page 47), this is a wonderful compliment to a light dinner or the mezze to a delicious feast. So dive right in, but DO NOT double dip!

- 2 large Italian eggplants
- ¾ cup + 2 Tbsp (215 mL) extra virgin olive oil, divided
- Kosher salt
- 2 cloves garlic, chopped
- 1 Tbsp (15 mL) lemon juice + more as needed
- ¼ cup (60 mL) tahini (for homemade, see page 36)
- ¼ cup (60 mL) fresh parsley leaves, chopped
- ¼ tsp (1 mL) ground cumin
- 2 pinches za'atar, for serving

Preheat oven to 450°F (230°C).

Split the eggplants in half and score the flesh. Brush ⅓ cup (80 mL) olive oil onto the eggplant flesh and season with salt. Line a baking tray with parchment paper and place the 4 eggplant halves on top, skin side up. Roast in the oven until the flesh is tender, about 35–40 minutes.

Remove the tray from the oven and let the eggplant halves cool for a bit, then flip them over. Place a mesh strainer over a mixing bowl and scoop the flesh from the eggplants into the strainer with a large spoon; discard the skins. You want to remove most of the moisture from the eggplants, so let them sit in the strainer for a few minutes, then stir to release additional moisture.

In a high-speed blender, add the eggplant flesh, garlic and lemon juice and blend until smooth. Add the tahini and emulsify by slowly adding ½ cup (125 mL) olive oil in a steady stream until you achieve a silky, pale and creamy texture. Fold the parsley, cumin and 2 tsp (10 mL) salt into the mix; adjust the balance if more lemon juice or salt is needed.

Serve in a bowl. Just before serving, sprinkle with za'atar and drizzle with ½ Tbsp (7 mL) olive oil.

Store in a sealed airtight container up to 3 days in the fridge.

GUACAMOLE

MAKES ABOUT 2 CUPS (500 ML)

3 avocados, pitted and diced

1 lime, juiced and zested + 1 lime cut into wedges for serving

Kosher salt

½ cup (125 mL) diced onion

1 clove garlic, minced

1 pinch cumin

¼ cup (60 mL) chopped cilantro

1 Roma tomato, cored, seeded and diced

Avocados are nature's butter. With a refreshing squeeze of lime, a few fresh herbs and a pinch o' spice, this is the perfect creamy accompaniment to a fresh plate of vegetables or a crispy bowl of root Vegetable Chips (page 56).

In a medium bowl, mash the diced avocados with the lime juice, zest and 1 tsp (5 mL) salt. Add the onion, garlic, cumin and cilantro and mix well. Adjust the seasoning with salt and more lime, if needed.

Place the guacamole in a serving bowl and mix in the diced tomato. Best enjoyed right away, as it doesn't keep well and will oxidize. Serve with lime wedges on the side.

CREAMY AVOCADO DIP

MAKES ABOUT 1½ CUPS (375 ML)

2 ripe avocados, pitted and cut into chunks

1 clove garlic, minced

¼ tsp (1 mL) sea salt

⅛ tsp (0.5 mL) fresh black pepper

½ cup (125 mL) unsweetened coconut milk

Avocado has been popular for years for good reason: it's delicious. This recipe takes only seconds to execute, then you'll be able to return to whatever you were doing with this creamy bowl of goodness to enjoy on the side.

Place all the ingredients in a high-speed blender with half the coconut milk and purée until smooth. Gradually add more coconut milk as you go, blending until you obtain the consistency you desire. Serve in a bowl.

TOMATO *and* SERRANO SALSA

MAKES ABOUT 1 CUP (250 ML)

True to its name, the flavours in this salsa will have your taste buds on the dance floor in no time. I recommend keeping the recipe for the summer months when tomatoes are in their prime—kissed by the sun and full of sweet goodness!

---

2 medium plum tomatoes, cored, seeded and diced

½ red onion, brunoised

2 serrano chilies, seeded and brunoised*

½ cup (125 mL) chopped cilantro

1 lime, juiced

1 pinch dried oregano

1 pinch ground cumin

Kosher salt

Fresh black pepper

In a medium bowl, mix together the tomatoes, onion and chilies; stir to combine. Add the cilantro, lime juice, oregano and cumin and season with salt and pepper to taste. Keep at room temperature and serve fresh.

NOTE: Be sure to wash your hands, knife and cutting board after cutting the hot pepper. Avoid any contact with your eyes for several hours.

---

* If you feel like adding more heat to the salsa, don't remove the seeds.

TAHINI DIP

MAKES ½ CUP (125 ML)

⅓ cup (80 mL) tahini (for homemade, recipe follows)

1 clove garlic, chopped

2 Tbsp (30 mL) lemon juice

1 Tbsp (15 mL) olive oil

Sea salt

3 Tbsp (45 mL) lukewarm water

1 pinch ground cumin

1 pinch cayenne

1 Tbsp (15 mL) fresh parsley

If you love tahini then this dip is for you—the perfect balance of heat, acid and bitterness, with a slight punch of garlic. Serve in a ramekin or small bowl as an accompaniment to Avocado Fries (page 59).

In a small bowl, whisk the tahini, garlic, lemon juice, olive oil and ½ tsp (2 mL) salt until combined. Whisk in the water, 1 Tbsp (15 mL) at the time. Stir in the cumin, cayenne and parsley. Adjust the seasoning with salt if necessary and serve.

HOMEMADE TAHINI

1 cup (250 mL) sesame seeds

¼ cup (60 mL) grapeseed or vegetable oil

1 tsp (5 mL) kosher salt (or more as needed)

In a dry medium saucepan, toast the sesame seeds over medium-low heat until completely golden brown, stirring constantly so they don't burn. Transfer the seeds to parchment paper and lay them flat, allowing them to cool completely.

Blitz the seeds in a high-speed blender or food processor until a crumbly paste forms, then add the oil and mix for another 2–3 minutes, stopping to scrape the bottom and sides of the food processor a couple times. Check the consistency, it should be smooth and pourable. Add the salt and pulse to mix it well.

Store in a sealed airtight container up to a month in the fridge.

ROASTED RED PEPPER HUMMUS

MAKES ABOUT 2 CUPS (500 ML)

For a long time I never really enjoyed hummus. The reason why, you ask? Mainly because I only ever sampled the store-bought kind. Thankfully, I had my world turned upside down when a bowl of hummus was served as part of a spread at a dinner I attended at an Israeli restaurant. After experiencing that, I raced back to my kitchen to recreate and perfect it, and I am happy to share my version of hummus here, with the addition of sweet red pepper. Serve with Pita Bread (page 47) alongside Baba Ganoush (page 33).

- 3½ Tbsp (52 mL) tahini (for homemade, see page 36)
- 2–4 Tbsp (30–60 mL) cold water + more as needed
- ½ cup (125 mL) extra virgin olive oil + 1 Tbsp (15 mL) for serving
- ½ tsp (2 mL) cumin + more as needed
- 2 cloves garlic confit
- Lemon juice, as needed
- ½ cup (125 mL) chopped roasted red pepper
- Kosher salt
- 1¼ cups (310 mL) dry chickpeas
- 2 pinches Espelette pepper, for serving

In a food processor, add the tahini, cold water, olive oil, cumin, garlic confit, lemon juice, red pepper and ½ tsp (2 mL) salt and purée until smooth. Add the chickpeas and purée for 3–4 minutes, pausing halfway to scrape down the sides of the bowl, until smooth. If it seems too thick, add in another 1–2 Tbsp (15–30 mL) water.

Adjust the seasoning as needed with salt, cumin or lemon juice. Cover with plastic wrap directly touching the surface of the hummus so it doesn't create a skin.

To serve, place the hummus in a bowl, sprinkle with Espelette and drizzle with 1 Tbsp (15 mL) olive oil. Store in a sealed airtight container up to 3 days in the fridge.

AQUAFABA MAYO

MAKES 1¼ CUPS (310 ML)

¼ cup (60 mL) aquafaba

¼ tsp (1 mL) ground mustard

½ Tbsp (7 mL) lemon juice

1 tsp (5 mL) maple syrup

Kosher salt

1 cup (250 mL) vegetable oil (or any neutral oil) + more as needed

½ tsp (2 mL) smoked paprika

Listen, I am French and let me tell you, we LOVE mayonnaise back home. I can eat it on bread, that's how much I love it. It's a great base for dressing, dips, and more. So how do we make it vegan? Aquafaba! This is the answer to so many questions when it comes to subbing for eggs in plant-based dishes.

Add the aquafaba to a 4-cup (1 L) plastic container or jar along with the ground mustard, lemon juice, maple syrup and ¼ tsp (1 mL) salt. Blend with an immersion blender on high, slowly adding the vegetable oil in a steady stream until emulsified. Move the immersion blender up and down to incorporate a little air towards the end. If it's looking too thin, add more oil. Add more salt if necessary then add the smoked paprika.

Use immediately or transfer to a sealed container and place in the refrigerator until cold, about 4 hours. It will thicken as it cools, and it keeps up to 3 days in a sealed airtight container.

MISO MAYO

MAKES ABOUT 1½ CUPS (375 ML)

1½ cups (375 mL) raw unsalted cashews, soaked overnight and drained

2 tsp (10 mL) miso

2 Tbsp (30 mL) apple cider vinegar

2 Tbsp (30 mL) yuzu juice

Kosher salt

I have a major obsession with Asian cuisines and their wonderful components, and miso is definitely one of my favourite ingredients to use. Miso is fermented soybean paste that is rich and salty and has a unique flavour I cannot get enough of, providing an explosion of umami when used properly. This recipe turns it into a mayo you will want to dip all your best bites into.

Place all the ingredients into a high-speed blender. Blend until completely smooth; you can add 1 Tbsp (15 mL) water if you're looking for a thinner dressing. Season with salt to taste.

Store in a sealed airtight container up to 5 days in the fridge.

PEBRE

MAKES 1 CUP (250 ML)

Imagine if a salsa and chimichurri had a child—its name would be Pebre, a spicy, sweet and herbaceous little one. Best enjoyed as a garnish, sauce or even as a snack with tortilla chips.

- ½ shallot, brunoised
- ½ jalapeno, seeded and brunoised
- 2 cloves garlic, minced
- ¼ cup (60 mL) red wine vinegar
- Kosher salt
- ¼ cup (60 mL) chopped cilantro
- 2 Tbsp (30 mL) chopped flat parsley
- 4 stalks oregano, leaves picked and chopped
- ½ cup (125 mL) olive oil
- 2 heirloom tomatoes, cored, seeded and diced
- Fresh black pepper

In a medium bowl, combine the shallot, jalapeno, garlic, red wine vinegar and ½ tsp (2 mL) salt. Marinate for 10 minutes, then stir in the cilantro, parsley and oregano. Emulsify by slowly adding the olive oil in a steady stream while whisking continuously. Add the tomatoes and adjust the seasoning with salt and pepper to taste. Serve fresh in a small bowl.

BREADS

POPPY SEED AND SESAME LAVASH
GARLIC AND HERB FOCACCIA
EVERYTHING AND THE BAGEL

SOFT AND CHEWY
PRETZELS
CLASSIC PARISIAN BAGUETTES

CLASSIC PARISIAN BAGUETTES

MAKES 2 BAGUETTES

- 3⅔ cups (910 mL) bread flour, divided + 2 Tbsp (30 mL) for dusting
- 1⅓ cups + 1 Tbsp (345 mL) water, divided
- 1 tsp (5 mL) instant yeast, divided
- ½ Tbsp (7 mL) kosher salt, divided
- ½ tsp (2 mL) malt powder
- 2 Tbsp (30 mL) cornmeal

Very little beats a fresh, soft baguette with a beautiful crust. It's the perfect starter to any meal, a carb-y midday snack or the perfect foundation for your go-to sandwich. This recipe yields two baguettes, perfect for six to eight people—unless you're like us, in which case it only serves one.

In the bowl of a stand mixer fitted with the dough hook attachment, mix 1 cup (250 mL) bread flour, ⅓ cup (80 mL) water, ⅓ tsp (1.5 mL) yeast and ½ tsp (2 mL) salt together for 5 minutes on medium-low speed until combined. Cover the bowl with plastic wrap and allow the mixture to rest at room temperature for 20 minutes.

Remove the plastic wrap and add the remaining bread flour, water, yeast, salt and the malt powder to the dough. Continue to mix on low for 5 minutes, then for an additional 8 minutes on medium-high speed or until the dough becomes soft and smooth. Form the dough into a ball, cover the bowl with plastic wrap and rest at room temperature for 1 hour until doubled in size. After an hour, punch down the dough to release the gas, form back into a ball, cover the bowl with plastic wrap and rest in the fridge for another hour.

Remove the dough from the fridge and unwrap. Divide the dough in half and shape each half into a loose rectangle. Working the dough horizontally, flatten out each rectangle using the palms of your hands, squeezing out any excess gas and air bubbles. Begin to fold the rectangles lengthwise in thirds (like folding a letter for an envelope) to form 2 long oblong shapes. Cover the dough with plastic wrap or a towel and let it rest for 15 minutes. Repeat the flattening and folding again, lengthening the dough, then seal the narrow ends shut by folding the dough an inch or two over the seams and pinching them closed.

Begin to work each length of dough into a long, thin shape, like a rope, working from the middle outwards and gently tapering the ends to form a baguette shape. If the dough becomes stiff and doesn't retain its shape once lengthened, rest for 10 minutes covered with plastic wrap or a towel to let the gluten relax before stretching again. The final length of each dough should be roughly 20 inches (50 cm).

Deposit the baguettes onto a parchment-lined baking tray and cover with plastic wrap or a towel, allowing them to rise one final time at room temperature for 60–90 minutes or until doubled in thickness. Mix together 2 Tbsp (30 mL) bread flour with the cornmeal and sift a thin, even layer over the tops of the baguettes. Use a sharp knife or razor blade to score the bread, making several long gashes along the tops of each baguette. This allows the baguettes to bake evenly and release any excess gas.

In order to create a crisp crust, you must create steam in the oven during the first bit of baking. To do this, heat the oven to 250°C (480°F) and place a shallow baking sheet on the bottom rack. Once the sheet is hot, carefully pour about ½ cup (125 mL) water into the tray to create steam, then drop the temperature to 230°C (445°F) and close the oven door. After 5 minutes, quickly place the tray of scored baguettes into the oven on the middle rack, baking for 18–20 minutes or until the baguettes turn a gorgeous golden brown.

Remove bread from the oven and place on a rack to cool completely.

GARLIC *and* HERB FOCACCIA

MAKES 10–12 SERVINGS

HERBED GARLIC OIL

½ cup (125 mL) extra virgin olive oil

2 cloves garlic, minced

5 sage leaves, chiffonaded

2 sprigs thyme, chopped

1 rosemary sprig, chopped

FOCACCIA DOUGH

4½ cups (1.1 L) bread flour

1⅔ cups (435 mL) water

1 tsp (5 mL) instant yeast

½ Tbsp (7 mL) kosher salt + extra for sprinkling overtop

½ Tbsp (7 mL) malt powder

1 Tbsp (15 mL) extra virgin olive oil

If you ever wondered what it would be like to eat an herb-covered, garlicky cloud, you've come to the right place. Moist and flavourful in every bite, this is one of my favourite recipes to watch people taste for the first time. First they savour, then they devour.

HERBED GARLIC OIL In a small bowl, add all the herbed garlic oil ingredients and stir to combine. Let the oil sit at room temperature to infuse while you prepare the dough.

FOCACCIA DOUGH In the bowl of a stand mixer fitted with the dough hook attachment, mix together all the focaccia dough ingredients, except for the olive oil, for 5 minutes on low speed, then for 10 minutes on medium speed, until the dough becomes soft and smooth. Add 1 Tbsp (15 mL) olive oil and continue mixing for another 2 minutes until the fat fully incorporates into the dough.

In a large bowl, form the dough into a ball and pour two-thirds of the herbed garlic oil overtop. Cover the bowl with plastic wrap and let it sit at room temperature for 1 hour until the dough has doubled in size.

With your hands, gently stretch the proofed dough to fit a parchment-lined 9- × 13-inch (23 × 33 cm) tray, then pour additional herbed garlic oil overtop (reserve 2 Tbsp/30 mL for later). Cover the tray with plastic wrap or a towel and proof again, at room temperature, for 1 hour.

Preheat oven to 200°C (390°F).

Evenly sprinkle the focaccia dough with salt and bake for 20–25 minutes, or until golden brown. For extra shine, brush the remaining 2 Tbsp (30 mL) herbed garlic oil on top of the focaccia as soon as it comes out of the oven.

PITA BREAD

MAKES 10 PIECES

Probably one of my favourite breads, pita is so versatile. It can be used as a vessel in which to serve other ingredients, or you can simply tear it up and dip it into some Roasted Red Pepper Hummus (page 37) or Baba Ghanoush (page 33).

1¼ cups (310 mL) warm water

1 Tbsp (15 mL) dry active yeast

2½ cups (625 mL) all-purpose flour

2 tsp (10 mL) kosher salt

1 tsp (5 mL) extra virgin olive oil

In a medium bowl, mix the water and yeast together until dissolved; let the mixture sit for 10 minutes to activate.

In a separate bowl, mix three-quarters of the flour with the salt and olive oil, then add the yeast mixture and remaining flour and knead the dough for 7 minutes. If preferred, you can use a stand mixer (with the dough hook attachment) on medium speed for 7–8 minutes.

Place the dough in a clean bowl. Cover the bowl with plastic wrap and allow the dough to rise until it doubles, about 1–2 hours depending on the temperature of the room.

Remove the dough from the bowl and divide it into 8 pieces, then flatten and roll each with a floured rolling pin. On a flattop grill or in a cast iron pan, cook the dough over medium-high heat for a couple minutes on each side. (Alternatively, you can bake the dough in a 230°C/450°F oven for 3–4 minutes, or until golden brown and puffed.)

Serve pita bread hot and fresh, or let it cool on a wire rack for later.

CORN TORTILLAS

MAKES TEN 6-INCH (15 CM) TORTILLAS

1 cup (250 mL) masa harina
¼ tsp (1 mL) kosher salt
¾ cup (185 mL) hot water

This recipe was a must-have in this book, and we use it in few different dishes like our Deep-Fried Tomatillo Tacos (page 142) and Sweet Corn and Tomato Chili (page 126). There is nothing like a fresh taco served in a warm tortilla. When I have the craving and can't make them myself, I always go to my friend Elia's restaurant for a fresh traditional corn tortilla.

Mix the masa harina and salt together in a mixing bowl. Pour in the water and stir to combine. Using the palms of your hands, knead the dough for a minute or two—it should feel smooth but no longer sticky, and you should be able to easily form a springy dough ball. (Based on the weather and quality of flour, the dough might be either too dry or too wet; you can easily adjust the mix by adding water or flour until you get the right consistency.) Cover the bowl with plastic wrap or a wet towel and let it rest in a warm place for about 20–30 minutes.

Once rested, remove the plastic from the bowl and form the dough into a ball about the size of a golf ball. Flatten the dough with a tortilla press (see note following recipe) or use a rolling pin to roll the dough out until it's about ⅛ inch (0.3 cm) thick and 6 inches (15 cm) in diameter (you can of course make it bigger or smaller based on the size you desire, just increase the size of the dough ball).

Warm a cast iron pan over medium-high heat and add the tortillas one by one, cooking for about 1–2 minutes per side. Once cooked, move the tortillas to a plate or tray and cover with a towel to soften them and retain their moisture. Serve immediately.

NOTE: If using a tortilla press, cut a plastic food-preserving bag in half and place it on the press. Place the dough in the centre of the plastic sheet and cover with the other plastic sheet half. Press the top of the tortilla press down to make one ⅛ inch (0.3 cm)–thick tortilla. If uneven, you can rotate the dough and press it again. Peel the plastic off of the press and repeat the process until all the tortilla dough is used up.

TIP: You can cut the tortillas into triangles and fry them for some crunch.

SOFT *and* CHEWY PRETZELS

MAKES 6 PRETZELS

The trick to a puffy, chewy pretzel with a deep crust is poaching it in an alkaline solution before baking. Easy and fun, this recipe will make you feel like you have an Auntie Anne's in your own home!

3½ cups (875 mL) all-purpose flour, divided

12 cups + 2 Tbsp (3 L) water, divided

2⅓ tsp (11.5 mL) instant yeast, divided

1⅔ tsp (8 mL) kosher salt

½ Tbsp (7 mL) malt syrup*

1½ Tbsp (22 mL) vegan butter

½ cup (125 mL) baking soda

Coarse sea salt

In the bowl of a stand mixer fitted with the dough hook attachment, mix together ½ cup (125 mL) flour, 2 Tbsp (30 mL) water, ⅓ tsp (1.5 mL) yeast and ¼ tsp (1 mL) kosher salt on medium-low speed for 5 minutes. Cover the bowl with plastic wrap and let it to rest at room temperature for 20 minutes.

Unwrap the bowl and add 3 cups (750 mL) flour to the dough mixture, along with the malt syrup, 1 cup (250 mL) water, 2 tsp (10 mL) yeast and ½ Tbsp (7 mL) kosher salt. Mix for 5 minutes on low, then for an additional 10 minutes on medium-high, until the dough has become soft and smooth. Add the butter and mix for a final 2 minutes on medium until fully incorporated. Form the dough into a ball with your hands. Cover the bowl with plastic wrap and let it sit at room temperature for 1 hour until the dough has doubled in size.

Remove the plastic, punch down the dough to release the gas and round it up again into a ball. Cover the bowl with plastic again and place it in the fridge for 2 hours or overnight.

Remove the plastic from the bowl and divide the dough into 6 equal pieces. Begin to work the pieces into long ropes, then twist the ropes into pretzel shapes and transfer to a parchment-lined baking tray. Cover the tray with plastic wrap and rest in the fridge for 30 minutes to allow the dough to firm up.

Preheat oven to 200°C (390°F).

Fill a large pot with 11 cups (2.6 L) water, add the baking soda and bring to a simmer over low heat. Drop each pretzel into the simmering water for 10 seconds per side, then use a slotted spoon to transfer back to the parchment-lined baking tray and immediately sprinkle with sea salt to taste.

Bake for 12–15 minutes, until a deep golden brown. Remove from the oven and cool on a wire rack.

NOTE: You can shape and bake the dough into long ovals for "pretzel baguettes" to use as sandwich bread. You can even switch up the garnishes with fresh herbs or vegan cheese, or make sweet pretzels by adding cinnamon and sugar!

* Malt syrup is a natural sweetener that adds flavour, conditions the dough and gives us the deep brown crust we love on our pretzels! If you can't get your hands on any, not to worry, this recipe still tastes delicious with it omitted.

EVERYTHING *and the* BAGEL

MAKES 6 BAGELS

3¼ cups (810 mL) all-purpose flour
1 cup + 1 Tbsp (265 mL) water
1 tsp (5 mL) malt powder
¾ tsp (4 mL) instant yeast
2½ tsp (12 mL) kosher salt, divided
4½ Tbsp (67 mL) malt syrup
1 Tbsp (15 mL) baking soda
6 Tbsp (90 mL) everything bagel seasoning, for garnish*

* Can't get your hands on store-bought everything bagel seasoning? No problem! Slap your own seasoning together by simply combining poppy seeds, white sesame seeds, black sesame seeds, salt, minced dried garlic and minced dried onion.

These bagels are so soft and chewy, you'll want them for breakfast, lunch and dinner. Perfect with a schmear of vegan cream cheese, your favourite fruit preserves or as an alternative to your usual morning avocado toast!

In the bowl of a stand mixer fitted with the dough hook attachment, mix together the flour, water, malt powder, instant yeast and ½ Tbsp (7 mL) salt for 5 minutes on low, then for an additional 10 minutes on medium-high, or until the dough becomes softer, pliable and smooth. Form the dough into a ball with your hands, cover the bowl with plastic wrap and let it sit at room temperature for 1 hour until doubled in size.

Remove the plastic and punch down the dough to release any gas. Form the dough back into a ball, cover the bowl with plastic wrap again and rest in the fridge for 2 hours or overnight.

Remove the dough from the fridge and divide it into 6 equal pieces. Round each piece into a smooth ball, place on a parchment-lined baking tray and cover the tray with plastic wrap; rest at room temperature for 20 minutes.

Remove the plastic and pierce a hole through the centre of each dough ball with your finger. Carefully begin to enlarge each hole, pulling and widening each opening to form your bagel hole. Cover the tray with plastic wrap or a towel and place in the fridge for 30 minutes to allow the dough to firm up.

Preheat oven to 225°C (440°F).

Fill a large pot with 10½ cups (2.5 L) water and bring to a simmer over low heat. Add the malt syrup, baking soda and remaining salt. Drop each bagel into the simmering liquid for 30 seconds per side, then use a slotted spoon to transfer back to the parchment-lined tray, sprinkling liberally with seasoning right away.

Bake for 12–15 minutes or until golden brown. Once baked, remove bagels from the oven and cool on a wire rack.

POPPY SEED *and* SESAME LAVASH

MAKES 8–10 SERVINGS

Thin, crispy, crunchy bites to bury into your favourite dips and spreads. These are easy to make, and require minimal ingredients from your pantry! Serve with Roasted Red Pepper Hummus (page 37).

- 1½ cups (375 mL) all-purpose flour
- 1 tsp (5 mL) kosher salt
- ⅓ cup + 2 Tbsp (110 mL) water
- ¼ cup (60 mL) extra virgin olive oil
- 1 tsp (5 mL) za'atar
- 2 Tbsp (30 mL) poppy seeds
- 2 Tbsp (30 mL) sesame seeds

In the bowl of a stand mixer fitted with the dough hook attachment, combine the flour, salt, water and oil and mix for 5–8 minutes on medium-low speed until smooth. Cover the bowl with plastic wrap and let it rest for 60 minutes at room temperature.

Remove the plastic and, without removing the dough from the bowl, gently fold the dough towards its centre. Flip the dough over so the folded-in edges are at the bottom and the top is smooth, then re-cover the bowl with plastic wrap and rest for an additional 30 minutes at room temperature.

Preheat oven to 200°C (390°F).

Remove the plastic from the bowl and divide the dough into 3 equal pieces. Flatten each piece with your hands or a rolling pin. Working over a parchment-lined tray, gently stretch and pull one of the pieces of dough until translucent and stretched out to the size of the entire tray. Sprinkle the za'atar evenly over the dough.

Bake for about 6 minutes, or until golden brown. Place on a wire rack to cool. Repeat this process with the remaining pieces of dough, sprinkling one with the poppy seeds and the other with the sesame seeds.

Once the sheets of cracker have cooled, gently break into manageable pieces, whip out the hummus and enjoy!

SNACKS *and* SIDES

GARLIC ROASTED CHICKPEAS

MAKES 1½ CUPS (375 ML)

1½ cups (375 mL) canned chickpeas, drained and rinsed

1 Tbsp (15 mL) extra virgin olive oil

1 tsp (5 mL) kosher salt (or more as needed)

1 clove garlic, crushed

½ lemon, zested

Sometimes you get that salty craving but you feel like your pantry doesn't have what it takes. Well, here's a quick snack you can make at the beginning of the week then keep on hand for future emergencies. It also goes great on top of salads like our Kale Caesar (page 92).

Preheat oven to 200°C (400°F).

In a large mixing bowl, toss the chickpeas with the olive oil, salt and crushed garlic until combined. Remove the chickpeas and place them in a single layer on a parchment-lined baking sheet. Bake until crispy, about 40–45 minutes.

Once cooked, transfer the chickpeas to a paper towel to remove excess fat. Toss them in a bowl with the lemon zest and mix together until combined (you want to mix the lemon and chickpeas together while still warm, to enhance the citrus flavour). Cool and store in a sealed airtight container up to 5 days in the fridge.

CRUDITÉ PLATTER

MAKES 4–6 SERVINGS

About 6–8 baby cucumbers, cut into quarters lengthwise

½ lb (225 g) cherry tomatoes

6 medium carrots, peeled and cut into batons

8–10 breakfast radishes, cut in half

½ lb (225 g) pickled green beans, drained and dried

2 red peppers, cut into batons

1 cauliflower, broken down into florets

6 radicchio leaves

Lemon wedges, for serving (optional)

Maldon salt, for garnish (optional)

Extra virgin olive oil, for serving (optional)

Replace your typical nachos and cheese with this vegetable-forward appetizer! For a stylish display, place dipping bowls filled with Artichoke Dip (page 32) and Spinach Dip (page 32) in the middle of the platter. These two dairy-free "cheesy" dips will pair perfectly with your favourite fresh vegetables—so go on and dig in!

Prepare all the ingredients as directed.

To serve, cover a platter with radicchio leaves to create a "bed." Place bowls of dip on top of the radicchio in the centre of the platter and arrange all the vegetables in bundles around them, trying to make the colours spark, with no identical colours side by side. You can also add some lemon wedges, sprinkle with Maldon salt and drizzle olive oil overtop, if desired.

CANTALOUPE *and* BASIL TWO WAYS

MAKES 4 SERVINGS

Take your summer melon snack up a notch by adding a fresh herbaceous bite to it! This recipe combines delicious cubes of infused melon and a shot of melon juice for a surprising and refreshing twist on a summer fruit favourite. It takes me back to my summers in France as a kid, picking melons from the field at the farm.

1½ ripe cantaloupes, seeded, divided

20 basil leaves, divided

10 basil stems

1 tsp (5 mL) extra virgin olive oil + extra for serving

Maldon salt

Cut the flesh of 1 cantaloupe into neat 1-inch (2.5 cm) cubes and reserve any trimmings. Finely slice 10 basil leaves and combine with the melon and 1 tsp (5 mL) olive oil in an airtight plastic bag or container. Chill overnight in the refrigerator to combine flavours.

Scoop the flesh from the other melon half and mix it with any leftover melon trimmings in the bowl of a food processor; blend on high speed until very smooth. Pass the puréed melon through a fine mesh sieve into a medium pot with the basil stems. Bring to a boil, then immediately remove from heat. Cover and chill overnight in the refrigerator.

Strain and discard the basil stalks from the melon purée and pour the mixture into small glasses; add a drop of olive oil and a sprinkle of Maldon salt on top of each and serve with eco-friendly straws. Place the melon cubes on 4 small plates and dress with the remaining basil leaves and olive oil.

VEGETABLE CHIPS

MAKES 3–4 SERVINGS

- 1 large carrot
- 1 large parsnip
- 1 taro root
- 1 sweet potato
- 1 Yukon Gold potato
- 1 large beet
- Vegetable oil, for frying
- 2 tsp (10 mL) kosher salt
- ¼ tsp (1 mL) garlic powder
- ¼ tsp (1 mL) onion powder

I'm going to be real with you—I am not a big fan of potato chips. However, this homemade selection of thin, deep-fried root vegetable chips is the perfect balance of earthy, crunchy, sweet and salty deliciousness. I suggest serving them in a wooden bowl with Guacamole (page 34) or your favourite dip.

Preheat oven to 95°C (200°F).

Wash and scrub (or peel) all of the vegetables, then thinly slice each with a mandoline to about 1⁄16 inch (1.5 mm). Transfer the slices to a bowl of ice water, except for the beet, which will need its own bowl as it will bleed. After 5 minutes, take the slices out of the water and place on a baking sheet with lots of paper towels; pat the vegetables dry to remove as much water as possible.

Fill a heavy-bottomed pan halfway with vegetable oil and heat to 175°C (350°F)—you can use a cooking thermometer to measure as you go. Fry the vegetables in small batches (so the temperature of the oil doesn't drop), ensuring the chips stay separated by breaking them apart with a spider or slotted spoon. Once crisp and golden brown, transfer the chips to a tray covered with absorbent paper to drain the excess fat. Season the chips as they come out of the oil with a blend of the salt, garlic powder and onion powder.

Transfer the fried vegetables to a baking sheet and bake in the oven for 5 minutes, just to crisp them completely. Remove chips from the oven and cool on paper towels to absorb the excess oil.

Add the chips to a serving bowl to be enjoyed right away, or place them in a sealed airtight container at room temperature for 3–4 days.

AVOCADO FRIES

MAKES 4 SERVINGS

Everyone loves a good avocado dish, but what if we fried it? Served alongside a delicious homemade Tahini Dip (page 36), you'll achieve a perfect balance of richness, bitterness and acidity with this perfect light bite.

- ½ cup (125 mL) fine almond flour
- ½ cup (125 mL) cornmeal
- ½ tsp (2 mL) paprika
- 1 tsp (5 mL) kosher salt, divided
- ½ cup (125 mL) all-purpose flour
- ½ cup (125 mL) almond milk (or any non-dairy milk)
- ½ tsp (2 mL) garlic powder
- 3 avocados
- 10 cilantro leaves, for garnish
- 2 limes, cut into wedges, for serving
- Tahini Dip (page 36), for serving

Preheat oven to 220°C (425°F).

In a medium bowl, add the almond flour, cornmeal, paprika and ½ tsp (2 mL) salt and stir to combine. In a separate bowl, add the remaining ingredients, except for the avocados and garnishes, and mix well (add more liquid if necessary, the batter shouldn't be too thin and should resemble pancake batter).

Cut the avocados in half and remove the skins and pits; cut each half into 4 equal slices. Using separate hands for the wet and dry mixes, dunk one avocado slice at a time into the wet mix and let the excess drip off, then place it into the dry mix to coat evenly. Place the coated slices on a greased or parchment-lined baking tray then repeat the steps with the remaining avocados.

Bake the avocado slices for 10 minutes, then flip them and bake for another 5 minutes. Remove the tray from the oven, arrange the slices on a platter and top with cilantro leaves. Place the lime wedges and Tahini Dip into ramekins and arrange the ramekins in the middle of the platter. Serve immediately.

AVOCADO *and* APPLE TOAST

MAKES 4 SLICES

- 2 avocados, pitted
- 1 Tbsp (15 mL) chiffonaded fresh cilantro + 12 leaves for garnish
- ¼ cup + 1 tsp (65 mL) extra virgin olive oil, divided
- 1 lemon, juiced and zested
- Maldon salt
- Fresh black pepper
- 1 shallot, diced
- 1 clove garlic, minced
- 4 slices sourdough (1 inch/2.5 cm thick)
- 1 red chili pepper, seeded and sliced
- 1 apple, diced into medium cubes

Avocado toast has been a trendy item over the past few years—and for good reason! This creamy fruit is the perfect plant-based spread for a morning slice of crisp toast. This recipe adds a unique and refreshing twist on the classic with sweet chunks of apple, spicy slices of chili pepper and refreshing cilantro leaves.

Scoop the flesh from the avocados, dice it and add it to a medium bowl. Add the cilantro, 2 Tbsp (30 mL) olive oil, lemon juice, 1 tsp (5 mL) salt, ½ tsp (2 mL) pepper, the diced shallot and the minced garlic and mash it all together. Adjust the seasoning if necessary.

In a large pan, heat 2 Tbsp (30 mL) olive oil over medium heat and toast the bread until golden brown (you can also toast the bread in a toaster or in the oven). Remove bread from the pan and spread with the avocado mixture. Garnish with the chili slices, cilantro leaves, diced apple, lemon zest, a little pinch of Maldon salt and a crack of black pepper. Drizzle 1 tsp (5 mL) olive oil overtop and enjoy.

FRESH THAI VEGETABLE ROLL

MAKES 12 ROLLS

I have been obsessed with Thai vegetable rolls since I first discovered them in a small Thai restaurant I used to stop by after work near Victoria station in London, England. I decided to recreate that memory and share it with you so you can also enjoy this wonderful dish yourself.

THAI ROLL

- 1 cup (250 mL) cooked rice noodles (follow package instructions)
- 1 tsp (5 mL) sesame oil
- ½ cup (125 mL) bean sprouts
- ⅓ head green cabbage, sliced thin
- 5 spring onions, chopped
- ½ cup (125 mL) peeled and julienned green mango
- 4 tsp (20 mL) shredded cilantro
- 4 tsp (20 mL) shredded basil
- 4 tsp (20 mL) shredded mint
- ¼ cup (60 mL) pickled carrot (recipe follows)
- 1 Tbsp (15 mL) lime juice
- 1 Tbsp (15 mL) San-J Tamari Soy Sauce
- 1 Tbsp (15 mL) pickled ginger (page 121)
- Kosher salt
- 12 Blue Dragon spring roll wrappers

DIPPING SAUCE

- 1 cup (250 mL) white sugar
- ½ cup (125 mL) water
- ½ cup (125 mL) white vinegar
- 2 tsp (10 mL) kosher salt
- 1 clove garlic, minced
- 1 bird's eye chili, minced

GARNISHES

- Lettuce leaves
- Lime wedges (optional)

THAI ROLL Toss the cooked rice noodles with the sesame oil. In a large bowl, mix the noodles and all remaining Thai roll ingredients, except for the salt and wrappers. Stir to combine, then season with 2 tsp (10 mL) salt and marinate for 5 minutes.

Submerge the spring roll wrappers in hot water until pliable (about 10–15 seconds). Place about 2 Tbsp (30 mL) of the veggie/noodle mix horizontally in the bottom of each wrapper, then fold the bottom half up over the filling and push down. Fold in both sides of the wrapper and gently press down. Continue rolling the spring roll towards the top of the wrapper. If it doesn't close properly, sprinkle the top with a bit of water to use as a sealant.

DIPPING SAUCE Combine the sugar, water, vinegar, salt, garlic and chili in a saucepan and bring to a boil. Reduce heat and simmer for 10 minutes. Remove from heat and cool to room temperature.

ASSEMBLY Place a few lettuce leaves on a flat dish and add the Thai rolls on top. Pour some of the chili sauce into a ramekin and place in the centre of the dish. You can add lime wedges on the side if desired.

PICKLED CARROT

In a medium pot, combine all the ingredients, except the carrot, and bring to a simmer over medium heat for 2–3 minutes.

In a medium bowl, add the julienned carrot and pour the pickling liquid overtop. Cool to room temperature before using and let it sit for at least an hour. Keep any extra pickled carrot in a sealed airtight container in the fridge. Shelf life: months.

- ½ cup (125 mL) rice vinegar
- ½ cup (125 mL) sugar
- ½ tsp (2 mL) coriander seeds
- ½ tsp (2 mL) cumin seeds
- 1 large carrot, peeled and julienned

LENTIL CABBAGE ROLLS *in* ROASTED TOMATO SAUCE

MAKES ABOUT 4 ROLLS

1 large white or green cabbage

TOMATO SAUCE

44 oz (1.2 kg) canned diced fire roasted tomatoes

2 Tbsp (30 mL) extra virgin olive oil

1 onion, minced

4 cloves garlic, minced

1 Tbsp (15 mL) tomato paste

Kosher salt

Fresh black pepper

¼ cup (60 mL) raisins

FILLING

½ cup (125 mL) dry lentils, cooked according to package instructions (using a veggie stock)

3 Tbsp (45 mL) dry bulgur, cooked according to package instructions (using a veggie stock)*

1 onion, minced

2 cloves garlic, minced

¼ cup (60 mL) finely chopped fresh parsley

2 tsp (10 mL) lemon juice

1 tsp (5 mL) smoked paprika

½ tsp (2 mL) cracked black pepper

½ tsp (2 mL) kosher salt + more as needed

¼ tsp (1 mL) allspice

GARNISHES

¼ cup (60 mL) flat parsley leaves

4 lemon wedges

*You can replace the bulgur with brown rice or quinoa, if desired.

Grab a little taste of Poland with this earthy and delicious traditional cabbage roll. I will let you in on a tidbit from our photoshoot: The entire team devoured these delicious rolls as soon as we were done.

Remove the core from the cabbage and freeze the leaves (this will make them easier to peel later). Once frozen, gently peel off the leaves until they become too small to use, then chop the remaining leaves and reserve for the tomato sauce.

Bring a large pot of salted water to a boil and prepare a large container of ice water. Blanch the leaves quickly in the boiling water to make them pliable, then shock them in the ice water and squeeze them gently to remove excess water. Place the leaves on a paper towel, pat dry and reserve for the rolls. (Note: It is important to remove as much water as possible.)

TOMATO SAUCE Blitz the tomatoes in a food processor until you achieve a thick, chunky purée. Set aside.

Heat the olive oil in a large Dutch oven–style pot over low heat and add the onion. Cook for a few minutes until the onion softens, then add the garlic and cook for another minute, stirring continuously. Add the tomato paste and cook for another minute, then add the puréed tomatoes. Season lightly with salt and pepper and cook for 45 minutes over low heat, stirring occasionally.

Remove pot from heat, add the raisins and reserved chopped cabbage and stir to combine. Cool for 15 minutes then reserve half the sauce, leaving the rest in the pot.

FILLING In a large bowl, combine all the filling ingredients together. Adjust the seasoning with salt if necessary.

ASSEMBLY Preheat oven to 175°C (350°F).

To fold the cabbage rolls, place a cabbage leaf on your cutting board with the concave side up and the stem facing towards you. Portion about ⅓ cup (80 mL) of the lentil mix near the stem and mold it in an oblong shape. Fold the stem up over the filling, then fold each of the sides towards the middle. Roll the filling up the rest of the leaf, making sure it's nice and tight. Repeat with the remaining leaves until you run out of mix or leaves.

Place the cabbage rolls on top of the tomato sauce in the Dutch oven. Spread the reserved tomato sauce over the cabbage rolls, cover with a lid and cook in the oven for 45–60 minutes, until the cabbage is tender. Stir often to ensure the sauce on the bottom of the pot does not burn.

Take 2 rolls and place in the centre of a plate, then cover with sauce. Add some chopped parsley overtop and serve with a lemon wedge on the side. Alternatively, just leave the rolls in the Dutch oven and serve as is. Enjoy them while they last!

BROCCOLINI TEMPURA *with* LEMON *and* CHILI OIL

MAKES 4–6 SERVINGS

Who doesn't love indulging in a plateful of crispy battered vegetables? This tempura has a spicy little twist that makes it oh-so-addicting. It's a sure-fire way to kick off your meal with a big burst of flavour.

CHILI OIL

2 red chilies, chopped (with seeds)

1 knob ginger, peeled and diced

½ cup (125 mL) grapeseed oil

BROCCOLINI TEMPURA

½ cup (125 mL) all-purpose flour

½ cup (125 mL) rice flour

½ cup (125 mL) corn starch

2 Tbsp (30 mL) baking powder

1 small bottle sparkling water

Vegetable oil, for frying

2 bunches broccolini, trimmed

1 tsp (5 mL) paprika

Kosher salt

2 lemons, cut into wedges

CHILI OIL In a small pot, combine all the chili oil ingredients and let them simmer over low heat for 30 minutes. Remove from heat and continue to steep until the mixture cools completely.

BROCCOLINI TEMPURA In a large bowl, mix together the flours, corn starch and baking powder. Slowly whisk some sparkling water into the bowl—the batter should be thin but thick enough to coat the broccolini.

Fill a deep pot two-thirds with vegetable oil and heat to 175°C (350°F). Dip the broccolini one piece at a time in the tempura batter then fry it in the oil until crispy, about 2–3 minutes. Once the batter is cooked inside and out, place the fried broccolini on a paper towel and season with the paprika and salt to taste.

Stack the broccolini nicely in a large coupe plate or bowl, add the lemon wedges and serve the chili oil in a ramekin with a teaspoon. You can also drizzle some chili oil on the broccolini.

CRISPY MEUNIÈRE-STYLE CAULIFLOWER

MAKES 4–6 SERVINGS

½ large cauliflower, cut into florets

2 Tbsp (30 mL) all-purpose flour

¼ cup (60 mL) non-dairy milk

½ cup (125 mL) panko or breadcrumbs

3 Tbsp (45 mL) nutritional yeast flakes

1 tsp (5 mL) kosher salt

Olive oil, for brushing

1 lemon, cut into wedges, for garnish

MEUNIÈRE SAUCE

½ cup (125 mL) vegan margarine

2 Tbsp (30 mL) capers

¼ cup (60 mL) finely chopped fresh parsley

Transform your cauliflower into a crispy, cheesy (but not real cheese) and totally crave-worthy dish. Breaded with a flavourful seasoning mix and served with a rich and creamy dip, this cauliflower floret shareable might be gone before it gets around the table!

Preheat oven to 175°C (350°F).

In a medium bowl, mix together the flour and non-dairy milk. In another bowl, mix the breadcrumbs, nutritional yeast flakes and salt. Start breading the florets by dipping them into the flour–milk mixture, then the bread mixture, until completely coated. Place the breaded cauliflower on a parchment-lined baking sheet and brush lightly with olive oil. Bake for about 30 minutes or until golden brown.

MEUNIÈRE SAUCE In a small pan over medium-low heat, melt the margarine and add the capers. Let it infuse for a couple minutes, then add the parsley and stir to combine.

ASSEMBLY Place the baked cauliflower in a nice deep dish and pour the meunière sauce overtop. Serve with lemon wedges.

ASPARAGUS *and* PUFFED AMARANTH

MAKES 4–6 SERVINGS

This crunchy, healthy side dish really pops (or should I say puffs) with flavour! Let your asparagus shine bright on the plate by adding a few light seasonings and a tart sherry dressing that's sure to excite and surprise!

PUFFED AMARANTH

- Vegetable oil, as needed
- ⅓ cup (80 mL) amaranth seeds
- Kosher salt

SHERRY DRESSING

- ½ Tbsp (7 mL) mustard
- ⅓ cup (80 mL) sherry vinegar
- ⅔ cup (160 mL) extra virgin olive oil
- Kosher salt
- Fresh black pepper

ASPARAGUS

- 2 bunches asparagus
- 3 Tbsp (45 mL) vegan butter
- ½ tsp (2 mL) garlic powder
- 3 Tbsp (45 mL) nutritional yeast
- 1 Tbsp (15 mL) extra virgin olive oil
- Kosher salt
- Fresh black pepper
- 1 lemon, zested
- ½ cup (125 mL) pea shoots, for garnish

PUFFED AMARANTH Fill a small pot two-thirds full with vegetable oil and heat it to its smoke point. Drop 1 Tbsp (15 mL) amaranth into the hot oil and let if puff. Using a tiny sieve, scoop the puffed amaranth out of the pot and onto a tray with absorbent paper to remove the excess fat. Season with salt and repeat the process until all the amaranth has puffed up.

SHERRY DRESSING In a medium bowl, whisk together the mustard and sherry vinegar. Emulsify by slowly adding ⅔ cup (160 mL) olive oil in a steady stream while whisking continuously. Season with salt and pepper to taste. Set aside.

ASPARAGUS Preheat oven 200°C (400°F).

Rinse the asparagus and snap off the tough ends; remove any thorns from the stalk using a paring knife and pat dry.

In a small pot over medium heat, melt the vegan butter. Add the garlic powder and nutritional yeast and stir to combine.

Place the asparagus on a parchment-lined baking sheet and drizzle 1 Tbsp (15 mL) olive oil overtop. Season with salt and pepper and drizzle with the vegan butter mixture. Bake the asparagus for 6–7 minutes.

ASSEMBLY Place the asparagus on a serving tray and top with the pea shoots. Drizzle with sherry dressing, top with puffed amaranth and sprinkle with salt.

CHARRED BRUSSELS SPROUTS

MAKES 4–6 SERVINGS

It's hard to believe there was a time when Brussels sprouts weren't very popular. Well, times have changed, and if you're still not a fan after this flavourful combo, you'll probably be the odd one out. Ever since I was little I have been a fan of the cauliflower family, and Brussels sprouts are no exceptions. One thing I would say, however, is that mine taste way better than the ones I used to eat at the cafeteria!

- 12 oz (340 g) Brussels sprouts
- 2½ Tbsp (37 mL) avocado oil
- 2 shallots, sliced thin
- 2 cloves garlic, smashed
- ¼ cup (60 mL) balsamic vinegar
- 1 lemon, zested
- Kosher salt
- 1 cup (250 mL) slivered almonds, toasted
- 5 stalks tarragon, leaves picked and chopped
- 1 jalapeno, seeded and sliced thin

Slice the bottoms off the Brussels sprouts and cut the sprouts in half. Wash thoroughly.

Bring a large pot of salted water to a boil and drop the sprouts in. Blanch the sprouts for 2–3 minutes, then remove them and shock in a bowl of ice water. Drain the water and let the sprouts cool completely on a sheet of absorbent paper.

In a cast iron or heavy-bottomed pan over medium-high heat, bring the avocado oil to just below its smoke point. Place the sprouts flat side down and char them for 2–3 minutes, then flip them and cook for another 1–2 minutes. Reduce heat to medium-low, add the shallots and garlic and cook until softened. Deglaze the pan with balsamic vinegar and reduce. Add the lemon zest, adjust the seasoning with salt and remove from heat. Add the almonds, tarragon and jalapeno to the Brussels sprouts and mix it all together. Serve in a large bowl and enjoy while hot.

COCONUT "CEVICHE"

MAKES 4 SERVINGS

Bring exotic flavours right to your dining room with this ceviche-inspired dish featuring four different interpretations of coconut! You'll feel like you're on vacation!

- One 400 mL can Blue Dragon coconut milk, refrigerated for 24 hours
- 2 young Thai coconuts
- ½ cup (125 mL) extra virgin olive oil
- ¼ cup (60 mL) lime juice
- ¼ cup (60 mL) coconut water
- 1 orange, zested
- 2 limes, zested
- 1 lemon, zested
- 1 Tbsp (15 mL) coconut sugar
- 2 tsp (10 mL) kosher salt

GARNISH

- 4–5 Tbsp (60–75 mL) diced pickled kiwi (recipe follows)
- 2 Tbsp (30 mL) cilantro cress (or regular cilantro leaves)
- 2 Tbsp (30 mL) red shiso cress (or red shiso leaves)
- Maldon salt
- Tortilla chips, for serving

Take the can of refrigerated coconut milk and spoon the fat into a separate container from the coconut water. Cover and reserve both ingredients separately in the fridge.

Split the coconuts into halves by smashing them with the back of a large knife while rotating to create a seam. Add the water from the coconuts to the water you collected from the can. Using a spoon, scoop out the flesh from the shells and slice off any shell still attached. Julienne the flesh then clean the shell and store it for later (see note following recipe).

In a medium bowl, mix the olive oil, lime juice, coconut water, citrus zests, sugar and kosher salt together and let them steep for a couple hours. Strain the liquid through a fine mesh sieve and reserve in the fridge.

ASSEMBLY Place dollops of coconut fat in the bottoms of 4 coupe plates or bowls. Layer the julienned coconut over top, add 2 Tbsp (30 mL) of reserved liquid per bowl and add some pickled kiwi. Garnish with cilantro and red shiso cress and sprinkle salt overtop. Serve with fresh tortilla chips.

NOTE: If desired, you can serve the recipe in a cleaned out coconut shell. Create a mound of salt in 4 deep bowls and place half a coconut shell on each mound. Place a dollop of coconut fat in each shell and build the recipe as above.

PICKLED KIWI

- ½ cup (125 mL) rice vinegar
- ½ cup (125 mL) coconut sugar
- 8 baby kiwis or 3 whole, peeled and diced

In a medium saucepan, combine the rice vinegar and coconut sugar and bring to a simmer over medium-high heat. Cook for a couple minutes, then transfer the mixture to a medium bowl and let it cool.

In another medium bowl, add the diced kiwis and pour the cooled pickling mixture overtop. Marinate for at least a couple hours in the fridge, uncovered. Can be stored for months in a sealed airtight container in the fridge.

Chef Elia Herrera
EXECUTIVE CHEF AND CO-OWNER, TECOLOTE

SMOOTHIES

MANGO MANIA TWIST
SMOOTHIE
NECTAR *of the*
PINK GODS STRAWBERRY
SMOOTHIE
ENERGIZING
CARROT *and*
ORANGE JUICE

ALL HULKED OUT
SMOOTHIE
ENTER *the* DRAGON FRUIT
BERRY SMOOTHIE

CHOCOLATE *and* BANANA BREAKFAST SMOOTHIE

MAKES 2 SERVINGS

2 cups (500 mL) almond milk (or your favourite non-dairy milk)

½ cup (125 mL) rolled oats

¼ cup (60 mL) almond butter

2 tsp (10 mL) flaxseed

3 Tbsp (45 mL) cooking cacao powder

Half the seeds from a vanilla pod (or ½ tsp/5 mL vanilla extract)

2 bananas, sliced (frozen is better)

1 pinch ground cinnamon

1 pinch kosher salt

2 medium scoops chocolate protein powder (precise measurement depends on brand)

½ cup (125 mL) ice (optional)

This smoothie takes me back to my childhood. Chocolate, banana and almond butter with oh-so-delicious nuts and seeds. Did I mention how easy it is to make?

Place all the ingredients in a high-speed blender and blitz until smooth. Pour into 2 tall glasses.

CITRUS *and* CANDY CANE BEET SMOOTHIE

MAKES 2 SERVINGS

2 clementines or tangerines, segmented

3 candy cane beets, washed, scrubbed and diced

1 banana, sliced

1 cup (250 mL) raspberries (frozen if not in season)

¼ cup (60 mL) roasted almond butter

2 Tbsp (30 mL) chia seeds

2 cups (500 mL) almond milk (or your favourite non-dairy milk)

Half the seeds from a vanilla pod (or ½ tsp/5 mL vanilla extract)

1 pinch kosher salt

The perfect combination of earthy and sweet beets with acidic and refreshing citrus. If you're looking to boost your energy level, this smoothie is exactly what you need.

Place all the ingredients in a high-speed blender and blitz until smooth. Pour into 2 tall glasses and enjoy right away.

MANGO MANIA TWIST SMOOTHIE

MAKES 2 SERVINGS

What's the twist? Sweet curry to spice up your life! The flavours in this smoothie blend seamlessly and complement each other in a bold way. Creamy and sweet, with a little kick—are you ready for it?

- 2 cups (500 mL) diced mango (Ataulfo or Alphonso, either fresh or frozen)
- 1 cup (250 mL) coconut yogurt
- 1 cup (250 mL) coconut water
- 1 Tbsp (15 mL) fresh lime juice
- 1 Tbsp (15 mL) goji powder (optional)
- 1 tsp (5 mL) ground coriander
- 1 tsp (5 mL) ground cumin
- 1 tsp (5 mL) ground ginger
- 1 tsp (5 mL) ground turmeric
- ½ tsp (2 mL) ground cardamom
- ½ tsp (2 mL) ground cinnamon
- ½ tsp (2 mL) ground cloves
- ¼ tsp (1 mL) cayenne pepper
- Dried mango slices, for garnish (optional)

Place all the ingredients, except for the garnish, in a high-speed blender and blitz until shiny and smooth. Pour into 2 tall glasses and garnish with dried mango, if desired.

NOTE: Goji powder is a great source of Vitamin A and a natural booster for glowing skin!

KIWI DAILY BOOSTER SMOOTHIE

MAKES 2 SERVINGS

This may be one of my favourite smoothies to date—it's the ideal recipe for a boost of vitamins to start the day off right. It also has only four ingredients, all of which are easy to find all year long. The secret is to find perfectly ripe kiwis.

- 3 ripe kiwis, quartered
- 1 ripe mango, peeled and diced
- 2 cups (500 mL) pineapple juice
- 1 banana, sliced

Place all the ingredients in a high-speed blender and blitz until smooth. Pour into 2 tall glasses.

NECTAR *of the* PINK GODS STRAWBERRY SMOOTHIE

MAKES 2 SERVINGS

2 tsp (10 mL) basil seeds

2 cups (500 mL) hulled strawberries (fresh or frozen) + 2 fresh sliced strawberries for garnish

2 bananas, sliced

½ cup (125 mL) soy milk + more as needed

2 Tbsp (30 mL) agave syrup

A standard classic and the most refreshing treat at any time of day. We threw some basil seeds into the party for an extra little health kick.

Soak the basil seeds in 1 cup (250 mL) warm water for 20 minutes until they swell, then strain.

Blitz the hulled strawberries, bananas, soy milk and agave syrup in a high-speed blender until smooth. Adjust with more or less soy milk based on your consistency preference. Garnish with basil seeds and fresh strawberries. Pour into 2 tall glasses.

ALL HULKED OUT SMOOTHIE

MAKES 2 SERVINGS

6 large kale leaves

1 Granny Smith apple

1 Golden Delicious apple

2 cups (500 mL) spinach leaves, packed

2 tsp (10 mL) ground flaxseed

2 Tbsp (30 mL) maple syrup

¾ cup (185 mL) soy milk

½ cup (125 mL) ice

This detoxifying smoothie is packed with vitamins and fibre to help free the inner energy monster in you. It's a great start to a busy day or a delicious end to an awesome workout.

Cut the stems off the kale. Core and roughly chop the apples, except for a quarter of the Granny Smith apple which can be reserved for garnish. Place all ingredients, except for the ice, into a high-speed blender and blitz until well incorporated and smooth. Add the ice and continue to blend. Pour into 2 tall glasses. If desired, garnish with the quarter of a Granny Smith apple sliced, fanned out, skewered and placed across the glass (see photo, page 79).

ENTER *the* DRAGON FRUIT BERRY SMOOTHIE

MAKES 2 SERVINGS

Naturally sweet, rich and vibrant in both flavours and colours, this smoothie elevates and highlights your favourite berries in an exciting way that's full of texture.

- 1 cup (250 mL) blueberries (fresh or frozen) + extra for garnish (optional)
- ½ cup (125 mL) blackberries (fresh or frozen) + extra for garnish (optional)
- ½ cup (125 mL) raspberries (fresh or frozen) + extra for garnish (optional)
- 1 cup (250 mL) vanilla soy milk
- 2 Tbsp (30 mL) cashew butter
- 1 Tbsp (15 mL) chia seeds
- 1 tsp (5 mL) dragon fruit powder* (optional)
- ¼ cup (60 mL) unsweetened shredded coconut
- Pomegranate seeds, for garnish (optional)

Blend all the ingredients, except for the shredded coconut and pomegranate seeds, in a high-speed blender for 3 minutes or until smooth. Add the shredded coconut and blend for an extra 30 seconds to incorporate. Serve in 2 tall cups and garnish with pomegranate seeds and fresh berries.

---

*Dragon fruit powder is full of vitamin C, nutrients and fibre and helps boost iron levels.

ENERGIZING CARROT *and* ORANGE JUICE

MAKES 2 SERVINGS

3 medium carrots, peeled and diced

¼ cup (60 mL) water

½ pineapple, cored and chopped

3 oranges, segmented and chopped

1 tsp (5 mL) fresh ginger, peeled and sliced

1 Tbsp (15 mL) lime juice

1 Tbsp (15 mL) agave nectar

Dried pineapple (recipe follows), for garnish (optional)

Vibrant and hydrating, this is just the boost you need to keep you and your immune system going and going and going . . .

Place the carrots in a high-speed blender with the water and blend until puréed. Strain the mixture through cheesecloth or an ultra-fine mesh strainer (this step will take a little while). Return the juice to the blender and add the remaining ingredients, blending until all the fruit is fully broken down. Strain and pour the smoothie into 2 tall glasses. Garnish with dried pineapple on top, if desired.

NOTE: If you have a juicer, simply place all ingredients in the machine and enjoy, no straining necessary!

DRIED PINEAPPLE

¼ pineapple, cored

Slice the pineapple horizontally into discs using a mandoline or sharp knife. Arrange the slices in a dehydrator at 57°C (135°F) for 3–4 hours, or if you don't have a dehydrator you can bake on a parchment-lined tray at 120°C (250°F) for 2–3 hours, checking every 20 minutes until the pineapple has dried out.

SALADS

MINTED PEA, ASPARAGUS *and* FAVA BEAN SALAD

MAKES 4–6 SERVINGS

5¾ cups (1.3 L) fava beans (either fresh or frozen)

4 cups (1 L) fresh English peas (frozen is fine when fresh are not in season)

12 stalks green asparagus, tough ends removed

6 breakfast radishes, sliced thin + extra for garnish (optional)

2 Tbsp (30 mL) lemon zest

2 cups (500 mL) baby arugula

12 mint leaves, chopped

¼ cup (60 mL) grated vegan Parmesan + extra for serving (optional)

Kosher salt

Fresh black pepper

LEMON DRESSING

1 Tbsp (15 mL) grainy Dijon mustard

⅓ cup (80 mL) lemon juice

⅔ cup (160 mL) extra virgin olive oil

Kosher salt

Fresh black pepper

So fresh and so clean, this salad screams spring and the rebirth of the soil after a long winter. Wow, I should be a poet...

Bring a large pot of salted water to boil and cook the fava beans for about a minute (you want to keep them crunchy and tender, so start with a minute and try them, then cook a little longer if needed). Remove them using a spider or a slotted spoon and plunge into a bowl of ice water to stop the cooking and fix the chlorophyll (preserving the colour of the beans). Repeat this process with the peas and asparagus, cooking one vegetable at a time.

Cut the cooked asparagus into 2- to 3-inch (5–8 cm) pieces.

LEMON DRESSING In a small bowl, mix the mustard and lemon juice together until smooth. Emulsify by slowly adding the olive oil in a steady stream while whisking continuously. Season with salt and pepper to taste.

ASSEMBLY In a salad bowl, mix the beans, peas and asparagus with the radishes, lemon zest, arugula, mint, vegan Parmesan and ¼ cup (60 mL) of the dressing. Season with salt and pepper to taste. You can add more radishes and vegan Parmesan on top for presentation, if desired.

SUMMER HEIRLOOM TOMATO SALAD *with* CRUNCHY QUINOA

MAKES 4–6 SERVINGS

Tell me what's better than a sun-kissed tomato that's crunchy, sweet and full of its delicious juices? This salad is so light and refreshing, and one of my absolute favourite things to eat in the summer.

1 cup (250 mL) uncooked black quinoa

Vegetable oil, for frying

Kosher salt

8 heirloom tomatoes (use multiple colours)

2 tsp (10 mL) fleur de sel

Cracked black pepper

¼ cup (60 mL) pine nut pesto (recipe follows)

1 tsp (5 mL) Monari Federzoni Aged Balsamic Vinegar of Modena

¼ cup (60 mL) micro basil (or regular basil)

Cook the quinoa according to the package instructions. When completely cooked (borderline mushy), strain and place on a dehydrator sheet and place into a dehydrator for 12 hours, until the quinoa has dried out completely. (If you don't have a dehydrator, you can use a parchment-lined baking sheet and place it in the oven on the lowest setting for 4–6 hours or until dry.)

Fill a medium pot two-thirds full with vegetable oil and heat to 175°C (350°F). Add the dehydrated quinoa until it puffs, then remove it and place it on a tray with absorbent paper to remove any excess oil. Season with salt to taste and cool.

Place the tomatoes either on a dish or a plate, alternating the colours from one tomato to the next. Season with fleur de sel and fresh cracked pepper. Drizzle some pesto over the tomatoes as well as balsamic vinegar and garnish with micro basil. Sprinkle the crunchy quinoa generously overtop.

TIP: Zest some lemon on top of the dish to brighten the dish even more.

PINE NUT PESTO

2 cups (500 mL) fresh basil leaves

1½ Tbsp (22 mL) pine nuts, toasted

1 clove garlic, diced

1 Tbsp (15 mL) lemon juice

1½ Tbsp (22 mL) nutritional yeast

¼ cup (60 mL) Colavita extra virgin olive oil

Kosher salt

In a high-speed blender or food processor, add all the ingredients except the salt and blitz until smooth; you should obtain a thick pourable liquid. Season with salt to taste.

KALE CAESAR

MAKES 3–4 SERVINGS

1–2 bunches black kale, spines removed, leaves massaged and chiffonaded

¼ cup (60 mL) Garlic Roasted Chickpeas (page 54)

¼ cup (60 mL) finely grated vegan Parmesan cheese,

SMOKY CAESAR DRESSING

¼ cup (60 mL) raw tahini

¼ cup (60 mL) water

2 cloves garlic, minced

4 tsp (20 mL) fresh lemon juice

½ tsp (2 mL) Dijon mustard

¼ tsp (1 mL) liquid smoke

Kosher salt

Cracked black pepper

Everything there is to love in a traditional Caesar is here—the iconic crunch of the salad and the creaminess of the dressing, with a bit of smokiness added in for a twist. It's a real delight! This is one of my favourite lunches—the perfect bite that isn't heavy but leaves you feeling full.

Prepare the kale and set aside in a large bowl.

SMOKY CAESAR DRESSING In a mixing bowl, combine the tahini, water, garlic, lemon juice, Dijon, liquid smoke, ½ tsp (2 mL) salt and ½ tsp (2 mL) cracked black pepper. Mix until smooth, and adjust the seasoning with salt and pepper to taste.

ASSEMBLY You can serve the salad in a salad bowl, or you can plate it individually. Mix the kale with the dressing and half the chickpeas in the bowl, then top with the leftover chickpeas and grated Parmesan to serve.

GREEN SALAD *with* LEMON DRESSING

MAKES 4–6 SERVINGS

This is my favourite lettuce blend, and I am letting you in on the secret. It features different textures and flavours—from sweet to earthy and bitter. Paired with an acidic lemony dressing it is perfect as either a side or as the base for a full meal.

½ head radicchio, broken down

½ head red leaf lettuce, broken down

½ head green oak lettuce, broken down

½ head red oak lettuce, broken down

½ head frisée, broken down

1 baby gem lettuce, broken down

Kosher salt (optional)

Fresh black pepper (optional)

LEMON DRESSING

½ Tbsp (7 mL) Dijon mustard

⅓ cup (80 mL) lemon juice

⅔ cup (160 mL) extra virgin olive oil

Kosher salt

Fresh black pepper

1 shallot, minced

Ensure all leafy greens are carefully washed and dried, then break them down. Mix all the greens together in a large bowl.

LEMON DRESSING In a small bowl, whisk the mustard and lemon juice together until smooth. Emulsify by slowly adding the olive oil in a steady stream while whisking continuously. Season with salt and pepper to taste and add the shallot.

ASSEMBLY Drizzle some dressing over the salad and combine, mixing with your hands or salad spoons to avoid crushing the greens. You can add a bit of black pepper and salt on top of the salad, if desired.

HERBED ROASTED POTATO SALAD *with* DIJON FRENCH DRESSING

MAKES 4–6 SERVINGS

1 lb (450 g) baby red potatoes

½ red onion, finely diced

1 cup (250 mL) chopped spring onions

1 red pepper, seeded and diced

3 stalks celery, diced

1 sprig rosemary, leaves picked and chopped

2 sprigs thyme, leaves picked and chopped

2 sprigs sage, leaves picked and chopped

DIJON FRENCH DRESSING

Boiling water, as needed

1 cup (250 mL) raw unsalted cashews

⅓ cup (80 mL) water

2 Tbsp (30 mL) apple cider vinegar

1 Tbsp (15 mL) Dijon mustard

1 Tbsp (15 mL) maple syrup

3 cloves garlic, crushed and chopped

1 tsp (5 mL) Tabasco

Kosher salt

Fresh black pepper

1 Tbsp (15 mL) extra virgin olive oil (or avocado or grapeseed oil)

Lemon juice (optional)

¼ cup (60 mL) chopped fresh dill leaves

GARNISH

1 lime, zested

¼ cup (60 mL) chopped parsley

Find me someone that doesn't like a potato salad and I'll show you someone who's never had it done right. This salad brings me back to my mom's kitchen—she used to make a version of this when we'd go for a picnic with the family on a sunny Sunday. I try to keep the recipe from going out of style.

Place the potatoes in a large pot of cold salted water and bring to a boil. Reduce heat to a simmer and continue to cook for 10–15 minutes, until potatoes are fork tender. Drain and let the potatoes cool to room temperature. Slice into equal-sized pieces (halves or quarters, depending on the size) and place in a large bowl. Add the vegetables and herbs and mix to combine.

DIJON FRENCH DRESSING Fill a small bowl with boiling water and submerge the cashews until softened. Drain well, then pulse the cashews in a high-speed blender with ⅓ cup (80 mL) water until smooth. Add the apple cider vinegar, mustard, maple syrup, garlic, Tabasco and salt and pepper to taste. Emulsify the dressing by adding the olive oil to the mix in a slow, steady stream while whisking continuously. If the dressing is too thick, add some lemon juice to achieve a thinner consistency. Adjust the seasoning with more salt and pepper and finish with the chopped dill.

ASSEMBLY Mix the dressing into the potato mixture until well combined. Serve in a mason jar or salad bowl and garnish with the lime zest and chopped parsley.

CHICKPEA POWER SALAD *with* GREEN GODDESS DRESSING

MAKES 4–6 SERVINGS

- 2 yams, peeled and diced to medium cubes
- 2 Tbsp (30 mL) coconut oil, divided
- Sea salt
- Fresh black pepper
- 14 oz (400 g) canned chickpeas, drained and rinsed (see note)
- ½ tsp (2 mL) cumin
- ¼ tsp (1 mL) ground cinnamon
- ⅛ tsp (0.5 mL) allspice
- 1 bunch black kale, spines removed, leaves massaged and chopped
- 2 Tbsp (30 mL) pumpkin seeds
- 2 Tbsp (30 mL) dried cranberries
- 1 Tbsp (15 mL) extra virgin olive oil
- 1 lemon, zested (optional)

GREEN GODDESS DRESSING

- 1½ ripe avocados, pitted and diced
- 1 clove garlic
- ¼ cup (60 mL) extra virgin olive oil
- ⅓ cup (80 mL) water
- 1 cup (250 mL) basil
- ¼ cup (60 mL) chopped parsley
- ¼ cup (60 mL) chopped chives
- 3 green onions (green part only), chopped
- 1 lemon, juiced
- 2 Tbsp (30 mL) apple cider vinegar
- Kosher salt

Craving a good, healthy salad, but also have to brave the cold winter? This recipe is exactly what you need to fuel up before stepping outside. The delicious herbaceous dressing will keep your taste buds in check as you pass the winter days.

Preheat oven to 175°C (350°F).

In a medium bowl, add the yams, 1 Tbsp (15 mL) coconut oil, ½ tsp (2 mL) salt and ½ tsp (2 mL) pepper. In a second medium bowl, add the chickpeas, remaining coconut oil, cumin, cinnamon, allspice and ½ tsp (2 mL) salt and ½ tsp (2 mL) pepper to taste; stir to combine.

Spread the yams out on one parchment-lined baking tray, and the chickpeas out on a second. Bake both trays until fully cooked, about 15–20 minutes (the yams may need longer, but be sure not to dry out the chickpeas). While the trays are in the oven, prepare the dressing.

GREEN GODDESS DRESSING In a high-speed blender, blitz the avocados, garlic, ¼ cup (60 mL) olive oil, water, herbs, green onions, lemon juice, apple cider vinegar and 1 tsp (5 mL) salt until smooth and creamy. Adjust the seasoning with more salt if necessary.

ASSEMBLY In a large bowl, mix the kale with the pumpkin seeds, dried cranberries and some of the dressing. Season with more salt and pepper to taste and place the salad in a deep coupe plate or salad bowl. Top the salad with the warm chickpeas and yams, drizzle with 1 Tbsp (15 mL) olive oil and sprinkle with sea salt. You can zest a lemon on top to add a bit of a zing, if desired.

NOTE: Canned chickpeas can be substituted with ½ cup (125 mL) dry chickpeas. If using dry, soak them overnight then cook in 1 cup + 2 Tbsp (280 mL) vegetable stock over medium heat until tender, about 15 minutes.

FIVE BEAN SALAD *with* DIJON MUSTARD DRESSING

MAKES 4–6 SERVINGS

From kitchen to kitchen, we can all appreciate a good ol' bean. Together, these five varieties create a protein-packed side dish that bursts with flavour to keep your taste buds tingling and your energy levels racing.

- 7½ oz (220 g) green beans, trimmed
- 2 cups (500 mL) canned red kidney beans, drained and rinsed (see note)
- 2 cups (500 mL) canned chickpeas, drained and rinsed (see note)
- 2 cups (500 mL) canned cannellini beans, drained and rinsed (see note)
- 2 cups (500 mL) canned black beans, drained and rinsed (see note)
- 3 scallions, finely diced
- 1 red pepper, seeded and brunoised
- ¼ English cucumber, brunoised
- ¼ cup (60 mL) finely chopped flat parsley + extra for garnish
- 1 grapefruit, segmented and sliced into thirds
- Kosher salt
- Fresh black pepper
- 1 lemon, zested

MUSTARD DRESSING

- 2 Tbsp (30 mL) Dijon mustard
- ⅓ cup (80 mL) lemon juice
- 2 cloves garlic, minced
- ⅓ cup (80 mL) extra virgin olive oil
- Kosher salt
- Fresh black pepper

Bring a large pot of salted water to a boil and blanch the green beans until cooked but still crunchy, about 3–4 minutes. Move them to a bowl of ice water to stop the cooking, then drain and place the beans on a paper towel; pat dry once cooled. Slice the beans into ½-inch (1 cm) pieces.

Mix the green beans together with all the other beans and add the scallions, red pepper, cucumber, parsley and grapefruit. Season with salt and pepper to taste and add the lemon zest; stir to combine.

MUSTARD DRESSING In a small bowl, whisk the mustard together with the lemon juice and garlic. Emulsify by slowly adding the olive oil in a steady stream while whisking continuously. Season with salt and pepper to taste.

ASSEMBLY Place the bean salad in a large bowl, adding height by making it nice and plump, then drizzle the dressing overtop. Garnish with extra parsley.

NOTE: Canned beans can be substituted with dry beans, just use a third the volume (in this case ⅔ cup/160 mL of each bean instead of 2 cups/500 mL), soak overnight and cook in 2 cups (500 mL) vegetable stock over medium-low heat until tender, about 15 minutes.

CITRUS *and* LENTIL SALAD

MAKES 3–4 SERVINGS

A salad is a mixture of colours, flavours and textures that come together to create something truly unique and special. Forget the leafy greens and opt for this colourful protein-packed salad bursting with citrus, fresh herbs and a subtle hint of spice.

- 1 cup (250 mL) uncooked green lentils, rinsed well
- 3 cups (750 mL) vegetable stock (for homemade, see page 114)
- 1 shallot, cut into quarters
- 1 bay leaf
- 2 cloves
- 4 sprigs thyme
- Sea salt
- ½ red onion, brunoised
- ½ red pepper, seeded and finely diced
- ½ green pepper, seeded and finely diced
- 1 carrot, peeled and finely diced
- ⅓ cucumber, seeded and diced
- 12 cherry tomatoes, halved
- ½ fennel bulb, diced
- 1 grapefruit, segmented and diced
- ½ cup (125 mL) chopped parsley
- 1 lemon, juiced
- 2 Tbsp (30 mL) extra virgin olive oil + extra for serving
- Fresh black pepper

In a large pot over medium heat, combine the lentils, stock, shallot, bay leaf, cloves, thyme and a couple pinches of salt. Bring to a simmer and cook uncovered until the lentils are tender but still have a bit of bite, about 15 minutes.

Transfer the lentils to a large bowl with the remaining liquid. Once cooled, drain the lentils and add them to another large bowl with the rest of the ingredients. Stir to combine and adjust the seasoning with salt and pepper to taste. Make sure the salad isn't packed and stays light and airy. Add a crack of pepper, salt and a drizzle of olive oil overtop.

KALE *and* QUINOA SALAD *with* MANGO DRESSING

MAKES 4–6 SERVINGS

- 2⅓ cups (580 mL) uncooked black quinoa
- 4 cups (1 L) vegetable stock (for homemade, see page 114)
- ½ onion, cut into quarters
- ½ carrot, peeled and chopped
- 2 bay leaves
- 1 Tbsp (15 mL) kosher salt
- 1 cup (250 mL) fresh mint leaves
- ¼ cup (60 mL) chopped fresh cilantro
- 1 chili pepper, seeded and sliced
- 24 roasted peanuts
- 1 large bunch black kale, spines removed, leaves massaged and chopped finely
- 12–16 sweet and spicy candied pecans (recipe follows)
- 2 Tbsp (30 mL) fresh coriander cress
- Crispy shallots (double the recipe on page 111), for garnish

MANGO DRESSING

- ½ mango, peeled and diced
- ¼ cup (60 mL) rice vinegar
- 2½ Tbsp (37 mL) lime juice
- ½ Tbsp (7 mL) brown sugar
- ⅓ cup (80 mL) mango juice
- Kosher salt
- ¾ cup (185 mL) olive oil

This salad is sure to please all the vegetable skeptics out there. It features a variety of textures, colours and spices that are so well balanced and full of flavour that it's sure to keep your guests coming back for more.

In a medium pot, combine the quinoa, stock, onion, carrot, bay leaves and salt. Cook over medium heat until tender, about 10 minutes, then remove the aromatics and cool.

MANGO DRESSING Combine all the mango dressing ingredients, except for the olive oil, in a high-speed blender and blitz until smooth. Move to a small bowl and emulsify by slowly adding the olive oil in a steady stream while whisking continuously. Adjust the seasoning and the balance of acid/sweet if needed.

ASSEMBLY In a large bowl, combine the quinoa mixture with all the remaining ingredients, except for the coriander cress and shallots; add some of the dressing and stir to combine.

Pile the salad up high in individual salad bowls. Place the coriander cress on top along with the crispy shallots. Add a pool of dressing to the side of the salad.

SWEET AND SPICY CANDIED PECANS

¾ cup (185 mL) pecans

½ tsp (2 mL) paprika

1 Tbsp (15 mL) maple syrup

½ Tbsp (7 mL) Dijon mustard

Preheat oven to 175°C (350°F).

Mix all of the ingredients together in a medium bowl and stir to combine. Spread the mixture on a parchment-lined baking sheet and bake until golden brown and crispy, about 8–12 minutes. Remove the tray from the oven and allow the nuts to cool, then break down the clusters.

ROASTED BEET SALAD *with* SHERRY DRESSING

MAKES 4–6 SERVINGS

My heart skips a beat every time I taste a sweet delicious beet, and after you try this roasted beet salad recipe I'm sure your heart will be jumping around too! I have always loved cooking with beets and have served many versions of this dish over the years at my restaurant.

- 3 cloves
- ½ tsp (2 mL) coriander seeds
- 2 long pepper catkins
- 6 medium red beets (skin on)
- 2 cloves garlic
- 2 bay leaves
- ¼ cup (60 mL) chopped parsley
- 1 tsp (5 mL) sea salt
- ½ tsp (2 mL) fresh black pepper

PICKLED FENNEL

- ¼ cup (60 mL) sugar
- ¼ cup (60 mL) apple cider vinegar
- ½ tsp (2 mL) fennel seeds
- 1 star anise
- ½ tsp (2 mL) coriander seeds
- ½ tsp (2 mL) kosher salt
- ¼ tsp (1 mL) fresh black pepper
- 5 stalks fennel

PICKLED ONIONS

- ¼ cup (60 mL) sugar
- ¼ cup (60 mL) red wine vinegar
- 1 long pepper catkin
- ½ tsp (2 mL) coriander seeds
- 1 bay leaf
- 12 red pearl onions, sliced in half

. . . ingredients continued

In a dry frying pan, toast the cloves, coriander seeds and long peppers for a minute or two over medium heat and slightly crush them.

Wash the beets and add them to a large pot with enough cold salted water to cover. Add the toasted spices, garlic and bay leaves and cook the beets on low until you're able to pierce them with little effort.

Remove the beets from the liquid and peel the skins off (this is easier to do while they're hot). Let the beets cool then cut them into large wedges and set aside.

PICKLED FENNEL In a medium pot, combine the sugar, apple cider vinegar, fennel seeds, star anise, coriander seeds, salt and pepper and bring to a simmer over medium-high heat. Once simmering, cook for 2 minutes, then remove from heat and steep for another 15 minutes. Allow the mixture to cool.

Thinly shave the fennel stalks with a mandoline, leaving the fronds intact; place the fronds in a bowl of ice water and reserve for garnish. Place the shaved fennel in a bowl and strain the pickling liquid overtop. Set aside. (Fennel suspended in pickling liquid can be kept for a few weeks in a sealed airtight container in the fridge).

PICKLED ONIONS In a medium pot, combine the sugar, red wine vinegar, long pepper, coriander seeds and bay leaf and bring to a simmer over medium-high heat. Once simmering, cook for 2 minutes, then remove from heat and steep for another 10 minutes.

. . . recipe continued

SHERRY DRESSING

1 shallot, diced

1 Tbsp (15 mL) Dijon mustard

⅓ cup (80 mL) sherry vinegar

1 tsp (5 mL) maple syrup

⅔ cup (160 mL) extra virgin olive oil

Kosher salt

Fresh black pepper

GARNISH

12 red sorrel leaves

1 small candy cane beet, sliced thin

¼ cup (60 mL) candied walnuts (recipe follows)

1 lemon, zested

Return the pickling liquid to a boil then strain it into a medium bowl over the pearl onions, making sure the onions are fully submerged. Cool to room temperature, then set aside. (Onions suspended in pickling liquid can be kept for a few weeks in a sealed airtight container in the fridge.)

SHERRY DRESSING Whisk the shallot with the mustard and vinegar, then add the maple syrup and stir to combine. Emulsify by slowly adding the olive oil in a steady stream while whisking continuously. Season with salt and pepper to taste.

ASSEMBLY In a medium bowl, combine the beets with the dressing and parsley and portion into individual plates. Garnish with a few pickled onions sliced into rings, the pickled fennel, red sorrel leaves, candy cane beet slices, some fennel fronds (as much as you'd like) and candied walnuts on top. Sprinkle salt, fresh black pepper and lemon zest overtop.

CANDIED WALNUTS

¼ cup (60 mL) walnuts

1 tsp (5 mL) paprika

1 Tbsp (15 mL) Dijon mustard

1 Tbsp (15 mL) agave syrup (or maple syrup)

Kosher salt

Fresh black pepper

Preheat oven to 175°C (350°F).

In a small bowl, stir all the ingredients together until combined. Spread the nuts evenly on a parchment-lined baking tray and bake until crunchy and golden brown, about 8–12 minutes. Remove from the oven and cool the nuts on the tray.

Store in a sealed airtight container in a dry storage area for up to 1 week.

"CHEDDAR" CHOPPED SALAD *with* RED WINE VINEGAR DRESSING

MAKES 4–6 SERVINGS

Your typical bowl of basic greens gets a mouth-watering makeover with a sweet and tangy dressing, a selection of refreshing vegetables and a generous handful of vegan cheese! This is such a delicious salad to have at any time of the day.

1 head romaine lettuce, broken down*

1 head red oak lettuce, broken down*

1 head radicchio, broken down*

½ red onion, julienned

1 stalk celery, diced

½ lb (225 g) cherry tomatoes, halved

½ red chili pepper, seeded and sliced thin

¼ cup (60 mL) chopped sun-dried tomatoes

1 cup (250 mL) canned chickpeas, drained and rinsed

1 cup (250 mL) cubed vegan cheddar

½ lemon, zested, for garnish

RED WINE VINEGAR DRESSING

1 Tbsp (15 mL) Dijon mustard

½ cup (125 mL) red wine vinegar

½ tsp (2 mL) maple syrup

2 cloves garlic, minced

2 stalks oregano, leaves picked and chopped

⅔ cup (160 mL) extra virgin olive oil

Kosher salt

Fresh black pepper

Mix all the lettuces together in a large bowl and set aside.

RED WINE VINEGAR DRESSING In a medium bowl, whisk the mustard with the vinegar, maple syrup, garlic and chopped oregano leaves. Emulsify by slowly adding the olive oil in a steady stream while whisking continuously. Season with salt and pepper to taste.

ASSEMBLY Dress the salad with the vinaigrette and combine, mixing with your hands or salad spoons to avoid crushing the greens. Portion the salad into salad bowls and layer the remaining salad ingredients evenly into each bowl, garnishing with lemon zest on top. Serve right away.

---

*Ensure all lettuces are carefully washed and dried before breaking them down.

COBB SALAD

MAKES 4–6 SERVINGS

1 head radicchio
1 head red leaf lettuce
1 head green oak lettuce
1 head red oak lettuce
1 head frisée
2 heads baby gem lettuce
1 cup (250 mL) fresh corn kernels
1 tsp (5 mL) vegetable oil
½ lb (225 g) white mushrooms, sliced
Kosher salt
Fresh black pepper
1½ cups (375 mL) cherry tomatoes, halved
2 avocados, pitted and sliced
½ red onion, julienned
Roasted tofu (recipe follows)
1 bunch chives, sliced, for garnish
½ lemon, zested, for garnish

SMOKY DRESSING

1 cup (250 mL) Aquafaba Mayo (page 38)
1 Tbsp (15 mL) Moutarde de Meaux pommery mustard
2 cloves garlic, minced
2 Tbsp (30 mL) tahini
1 Tbsp (15 mL) white wine vinegar
2 Tbsp (30 mL) lemon juice
1 Tbsp (15 mL) maple syrup
¼ cup (60 mL) nutritional yeast
1 tsp (5 mL) onion powder
½ tsp (2 mL) garlic powder
½ tsp (2 mL) liquid smoke
1 tsp (5 mL) kosher salt
4 stalks fresh dill, chopped
2 oz (60 g) tofu, pressed and crumbled

This mix of leafy greens is anything but ordinary! Topped with beautifully roasted chunks of tofu, a wide variety of your favourite fresh summer vegetables and a smoky, creamy vegan dressing, this salad is one that'll have even the carnivores begging for more!

Ensure all the leafy greens and lettuces are carefully washed and dried, then break them down and mix together in a large bowl. Set aside.

Bring a medium pot full of salted water to a boil. Blanch the corn kernels for 1 minute (or until cooked), then shock in a bowl of ice water for 5 minutes. Drain the water and place the corn on a tray covered in absorbent paper. Set aside.

In a large pan, heat the vegetable oil over high heat. Once the oil starts to shimmer, add the sliced mushrooms, season with salt and pepper to taste and cook until golden brown and tender. Remove from heat and allow the mushrooms to cool.

SMOKY DRESSING In a medium stainless steel bowl, add all the smoky dressing ingredients, except for the tofu, and whisk until smooth. Add the crumbled tofu and fold it in gently.

ASSEMBLY Mix the lettuces with some of the dressing. Plate the salad elegantly in individual salad bowls and sprinkle the cherry tomatoes, corn kernels, avocado, red onion and cooked mushrooms overtop. Add roasted tofu on top of each salad and drizzle with more dressing. Garnish with chives and lemon zest. You are now ready for my vegan Cobb experience.

ROASTED TOFU

Preheat oven to 200°C (400°F).

Whisk all the ingredients together, except for the tofu, then toss in the tofu and stir to combine. Line a baking sheet with parchment paper and lay the tofu chunks on top. Bake for 15 minutes or until golden brown. Keep warm until ready to serve.

2 Tbsp (30 mL) nutritional yeast

1 Tbsp (15 mL) extra virgin olive oil

1 Tbsp (15 mL) soy sauce

½ tsp (2 mL) garlic powder

12 oz (340 g) extra firm tofu, broken into chunks

SQUASH, POMEGRANATE *and* FRISÉE SALAD *with* LEMON-ROSEMARY VINAIGRETTE

MAKES 4 SERVINGS

When we first created this recipe, one of my chefs, Milo, was trying to understand my vision for the dish. I kept telling him that it was a salad and a composed dish at the same time. I could tell by the way he looked at me that I wasn't making any sense, but in the end we managed to develop this incredibly delicious meal!

This recipe is definitely a bit more complex, but we also wanted to provide you with some restaurant-quality dishes. We hope you'll experience its unique mix of flavours and textures for yourself.

---

1 head frisée, broken down

½ head radicchio, broken down

¼ cup (60 mL) pomegranate seeds

Kosher salt

Fresh black pepper

20 red shiso cress leaves and stems, for garnish (optional)

PRESERVED LEMON SYRUP

1¼ cups (310 mL) preserved lemon rinds (store-bought)

¼ cup (60 mL) water

⅓ cup (80 mL) sugar

LEMON-ROSEMARY VINAIGRETTE

⅔ cup (160 mL) lemon juice

¼ cup (60 mL) pomegranate syrup

¼ tsp (1 mL) xanthan gum

1 tsp (5 mL) kosher salt

½ cup (125 mL) rosemary oil (recipe follows)

SQUASH CURLS

Medium-sized butternut squash bottom (the round base with the seeds inside)*

1 tsp (5 mL) extra virgin olive oil

¼ tsp (1 mL) lemon juice

½ orange, zested

1 tsp (5 mL) kosher salt

. . . ingredients continued

In a large bowl, mix together the leaves from the frisée and radicchio with the pomegranate seeds and set aside.

PRESERVED LEMON SYRUP Wash the rinds of the preserved lemons. In a small pot over medium heat, add the rinds, water and sugar. Simmer for 10 minutes, remove from heat and strain. Set the lemons aside.

LEMON-ROSEMARY VINAIGRETTE In a large measuring cup, combine all the lemon-rosemary vinaigrette ingredients, except for the oil. Blitz with an immersion blender until smooth. Once smooth, emulsify by slowly whisking the rosemary oil into the measuring cup in a steady stream until fully combined.

SQUASH CURLS Remove the round base (seeded part) from the butternut squash. Using a spoon, scoop the seeds out and thinly slice the squash using a mandoline (it should be paper thin). Reserve any leftover squash for the purée.

Place the squash curls and all remaining squash curl ingredients into a vacuum seal bag and cook in a circulator at 85°C (185°F) for 10–12 minutes. (If you do not have a circulator or vacuum sealer, place the vacuum seal bag in a large pot of water and cook over low heat until soft, about 15–20 minutes.)

. . . recipe continued

SQUASH MEDALLIONS

Medium-sized butternut squash top (the straight part without seeds)*

1 Tbsp (15 mL) orange juice

1 tsp (5 mL) extra virgin olive oil

¼ orange, zested

2 sprigs thyme

SQUASH MEDALLIONS Remove the top part of the squash and slice it into 1-inch (2.5 cm) thick medallions/wedges. Using a 2-inch (5 cm) wide ring cutter, punch discs out of the slices (or cut into squares if you don't have a ring cutter). Reserve any leftover squash for the purée.

Place the squash and the remaining squash medallion ingredients into a vacuum seal bag and cook in a circulator at 85°C (185°F) for 20–30 minutes. (If you do not have a circulator or vacuum sealer, just cook everything in a large shallow pot, doubling the orange juice and olive oil and cooking everything at a simmer until nice and soft.)

SQUASH PURÉE

¼ orange, zested

¼ tsp (1 mL) black peppercorns

¼ tsp (1 mL) coriander seeds

1 clove

2 sprigs thyme

1 bay leaf

¼ cinnamon stick

1½ Tbsp (22 mL) extra virgin olive oil

7 oz (200 g) butternut squash, diced*

Kosher salt

Fresh black pepper

3½ Tbsp (52 mL) vegetable stock (for homemade, see page 114)

Lemon juice, as needed

SQUASH PURÉE Fill a sachet (you can use a really large tea bag, or make your own with cheesecloth) with the orange zest, peppercorns, coriander seeds, clove, thyme, bay leaf and cinnamon stick. Heat the olive oil in a sauté pan over medium heat and add the squash. Season with ½ tsp (2 mL) salt and ¼ tsp (1 mL) pepper to taste and sweat for few minutes without browning. Add the vegetable stock to the pan along with the sachet and cook over medium-low until reduced and nearly dry.

Remove the sachet and blend the squash in a food processor on high speed. Pass the mix through a sieve using a spatula to push it through. Season to taste with salt and lemon juice.

ASSEMBLY Cut the squash medallions in half and place each half side-by-side on a coupe plate, placing one medallion slightly higher than the other (see image, page 108). Drizzle 1 tsp (5 mL) of the preserved lemon syrup over the medallions and add a dollop of squash purée on top of each.

Combine the lettuces with the vinaigrette. Add salt and pepper to taste and mix gently, then place the salad to the left of the squash. Add the squash curls on top of the salad and finish by garnishing with red shiso cress.

*You'll only need 1 medium-sized butternut squash for the recipe, divided between different steps.

ROSEMARY OIL

2 cups (500 mL) olive oil

5 sprigs rosemary

In a medium pot, add the olive oil and rosemary and bring to a simmer over low heat, then remove from heat and let steep for a couple of hours at room temperature. This recipe works with many different flavours—try garlic, lemon, thyme, sage, oregano or chili, to name a few.

GREEN BEAN SALAD *with* CHAMPAGNE DRESSING

MAKES 4–6 SERVINGS

Craving a bite of some mean green beans? These sweet green beans are elevated with a drizzle of Dijon, a dash of chili flakes and a crispy onion garnish—the perfect accompaniment for any occasion!

1 lb (450 g) green beans, trimmed

1 shallot, brunoised

1 lemon, zested

Kosher salt

Fresh black pepper

CHAMPAGNE DRESSING

1 Tbsp (15 mL) Dijon mustard

2 Tbsp (30 mL) champagne vinegar

¼ cup (60 mL) extra virgin olive oil

Kosher salt

Fresh black pepper

GARNISH

2 tsp (10 mL) chili flakes

¼ cup (60 mL) crispy shallots (recipe follows)

1 cup (250 mL) pea shoots

Bring a large pot of salted water to a boil and blanch the green beans in batches until tender, about 3–4 minutes. Once cooked, place the beans in a bowl of ice water and, as soon as they are cold, remove from the water and pat dry (the longer they sit in water, the more flavours and nutrients they will lose). Cut the beans in half and set aside in a bowl.

CHAMPAGNE DRESSING In a small bowl, whisk the mustard and vinegar together. Emulsify by slowly adding the olive oil in a steady stream while whisking continuously. Season with salt and pepper to taste.

ASSEMBLY In a large bowl, mix the beans with some of the dressing and add the shallot and lemon zest. Adjust the salt and pepper to taste.

Serve the salad in a large bowl and garnish with the chili flakes and crispy shallots. Add the pea shoots on top. Serve the extra dressing on the side.

CRISPY SHALLOTS

Vegetable oil, for frying

2 Tbsp (30 mL) rice flour

1 shallot, sliced into rings

Kosher salt

Add about 2 inches (5 cm) vegetable oil to a Dutch oven and heat to 175°C (350°F). Add the rice flour to a bowl; dredge the shallot rings in the rice flour, then, working in small batches so they don't stick to one another, fry them in the oil. Once they're golden brown and crispy, remove the rings with a slotted spoon and place on a paper towel. Season with salt right away. Repeat the process until all the rings are fried.

SOUPS *and* ONE-POT MEALS

VEGETABLE STOCK

MAKES 8 CUPS (2 L)

¼ cup (60 mL) vegetable oil
1 onion, chopped
4 stalks celery, chopped
4 carrots, peeled and chopped
1 fennel bulb, chopped
4 cloves garlic, crushed
Vegetable peels and scraps*
¼ cup (60 mL) tomato paste
3 Tbsp (45 mL) nutritional yeast
½ tsp (2 mL) kosher salt
½ tsp (2 mL) fresh black pepper
8 cups (2 L) water
1 cup (250 mL) kale, stalks removed and leaves chiffonaded
½ cup (125 mL) parsley (with stalks)
4 sprigs thyme
2 sprigs rosemary
2 bay leaves

*These can be collected over time from other recipes and stored in the freezer in a reusable bag until needed.

Why add water when you can use a delicious vegetable broth? You're going to use this recipe a lot not just in our dishes but for everything you cook moving forward—it's way better than the store-bought variety plus it's full of nutrients, low in sodium and the best way to use up scraps you would otherwise throw out. You can also freeze it so that it's ready all year round.

Heat the vegetable oil in a soup pot over high heat. Add the onion, celery, carrots, fennel, garlic and peels and scraps and cook for 5–10 minutes, stirring frequently. Lower the heat and add the tomato paste and nutritional yeast; cook for 2 minutes, stirring occasionally. Add the remaining ingredients and bring to a boil, then lower heat and simmer, uncovered, for 30 minutes.

Strain and cool down as fast as possible in the fridge or freezer. Pour the stock into jars and store up to 1 week in the fridge. Alternatively, you can fill ice cube trays with stock and freeze them, which is a great way to add flavour to dishes, plus it's easy to store.

NOTE: To make fortified vegetable stock, simply cook the stock a second time over low heat for about 30 minutes until reduced by half.

MINESTRONE

MAKES 4–6 SERVINGS

Not only is this recipe absolutely stunning thanks to the natural colours of its ingredients, but it is also packed with nutrients and bright flavours. One serving of this soup is sure to add a little joy to those long fall and winter days.

3 Tbsp (45 mL) extra virgin olive oil + extra for serving

1 onion, diced

2 medium carrots, peeled and chopped

2 stalks celery, diced

¼ cup (60 mL) tomato paste

Kosher salt

Fresh black pepper

4 cloves garlic, minced

1 zucchini, diced

½ lb (225 g) green beans, trimmed and cut into 1-inch (2.5 cm) pieces

1 medium russet potato, peeled and diced

1 stalk oregano, leaves picked and chopped

2 stalks thyme, leaves picked and chopped

One 28 oz (794 g) can peeled San Marzano tomatoes, diced

4 cups (1 L) vegetable stock (for homemade, see page 114)

2 cups (500 mL) water

2 bay leaves

One 15 oz (425 g) can cannellini beans, drained and rinsed

2 cups (500 mL) collard greens, stalks removed and leaves chopped

2 tsp (10 mL) lemon juice

2 cups (500 mL) cooked vegan short pasta (follow package instructions)

20 flat parsley leaves, chiffonaded, for garnish

1 pinch Maldon salt, for garnish

1 pinch red chili flakes, for garnish

Heat the oil in a large pot over medium-high heat. Add the onion, carrots, celery and tomato paste and cook, stirring often, until all the vegetables soften. Season lightly with salt and pepper. Add the garlic, zucchini, green beans, potato, chopped oregano leaves and thyme and cook for about 2 minutes more.

Add the diced tomatoes (with their juices) along with the stock and water. Add the bay leaves and season with ½ tsp (2 mL) black pepper and 2 tsp (10 mL) salt, then bring to a simmer over medium-low heat. Cover with a lid, leaving a 1-inch (2.5 cm) gap for the steam to escape, and cook for 15 minutes. Remove the lid, add the cannellini beans and chopped collard green leaves and cook for another 10 minutes.

Remove pot from heat and discard the bay leaves. Stir in the lemon juice and adjust the seasoning with salt and pepper to taste.

Place an even portion of pasta in the bottom of 4–6 soup bowls and pour the soup overtop. Garnish with fresh parsley leaves and sprinkle with Maldon salt and chili flakes. Finish with a drizzle of extra virgin olive oil.

VEGAN VICHYSSOISE

MAKES 4–6 SERVINGS

Thick, creamy, sweet and comforting . . . this bowl is a year-round crowd pleaser. Whether you're sitting out in a pumpkin patch or cozying up next to the fireplace, this soup is guaranteed to bring a smile to the table! I truly believe this adapted classic recipe is going to win you over, just make sure all the veggies are thoroughly washed before you start, as they can get really sandy.

- 1 Tbsp (15 mL) extra virgin olive oil
- 2½ tsp (12 mL) vegan butter
- ½ onion, diced
- 2 large leeks, sliced thin*
- 3 russet potatoes, peeled and cubed
- 3 cloves garlic, minced
- 5 sprigs thyme, chopped
- 2 sprigs rosemary, chopped
- ¼ tsp (1 mL) ground coriander
- 3½ cups (875 mL) vegetable stock (for homemade, see page 114)
- 1 bay leaf
- Kosher salt
- Fresh black pepper
- ¾ cup (185 mL) coconut milk (or other non-dairy milk)
- ½ lemon, juiced
- 2 cups (500 mL) garlic croutons (recipe follows)
- ½ cup (125 mL) chopped chives, for garnish
- 1 cup (250 mL) sliced green onions, for garnish

In a large pot, heat the oil and vegan butter over medium heat. Add the onion and leeks and sweat without browning. Add the potatoes, garlic, thyme, rosemary and ground coriander and sauté for 2–3 minutes. Add the vegetable stock and bay leaf and season with 2 tsp (10 mL) salt and ½ tsp (2 mL) pepper. Bring to a simmer and cook for about 15–20 minutes, or until the potatoes are cooked.

Remove pot from heat, discard the bay leaf and add the coconut milk and lemon juice. Adjust the seasoning with salt and pepper to taste.

In a high-speed blender, pulse the soup until smooth and creamy; pass through a sieve to remove any excess fibres from the leeks.

Fill soup bowls two-thirds with soup and add croutons overtop. Garnish with chives and green onions.

GARLIC CROUTONS

- ¼ cup (60 mL) extra virgin olive oil
- 2 cloves garlic, smashed
- 2 cups (500 mL) diced bread (cut into small cubes)
- Kosher salt
- Fresh black pepper

In a frying pan, heat the oil over medium-high heat and add the smashed garlic. Add the diced bread and fry until crispy, about 2–3 minutes; season with salt and pepper. Place the bread on a paper towel to absorb the excess fat.

*You can reserve the green tops in a reusable bag and store in the freezer to make stock (see page 114).

SICILIAN TOMATO SOUP

MAKES 4–6 SERVINGS

- 1 Tbsp (15 mL) grapeseed oil
- 1 onion, chopped
- 1 shallot, chopped
- 2 cloves garlic, crushed + 2 cloves for the bread
- 1 bay leaf
- 14 basil leaves, divided
- 2 stalks fresh oregano, leaves picked and chopped
- Kosher salt
- One 28 oz (794 g) can peeled San Marzano tomatoes
- 3 russet potatoes, peeled and diced
- 2 Tbsp (30 mL) coconut sugar
- 2 cups (500 mL) fortified vegetable stock (see note page 114)
- ¼ cup (60 mL) sherry vinegar
- 4 slices sourdough bread, baked or toasted, for serving
- Fleur de sel, for serving
- Extra virgin olive oil, for serving

Take yourself back to the good old days of enjoying a big bowl of your mother's classic tomato soup. With a side of garlicky sourdough, this soup and bread combo is sure to make your heart and tummy smile!

Heat the grapeseed oil in a thick-bottomed pot over medium heat. Add the onion, shallot and garlic and cook until they start to sweat. Add the bay leaf, 10 basil leaves and oregano and cook until the onion is completely cooked and appears soft and translucent. Season with 2 tsp (10 mL) salt to taste.

Add the San Marzano tomatoes (with their juices), diced potatoes, coconut sugar and fortified stock. Bring to a simmer over medium-low heat and cook for about 30 minutes while the flavours infuse.

In a food processor, blend the soup in batches until smooth. Season with vinegar and salt to taste.

Rub 2 cloves of garlic on the slices of sourdough (you can either toast them in a pan with olive oil or bake them in the oven) to serve alongside the soup. Chiffonade the remaining 4 basil leaves. Pour the soup into bowls and garnish with the basil chiffonade. Finish with fleur de sel and olive oil.

COCONUT GINGER SQUASH SOUP

MAKES 4–6 SERVINGS

I created this soup a few years ago for the soup festival in Toronto during an especially cold and damp "chilling your bones" kind of fall. I needed to create something warm and spicy to counter the gloomy weather, and squash was in season. The results were such a crowd pleaser that I went on to serve it at the restaurant I was working for. It was really hard for me to eventually take it off the menu as guests were absolutely in love with it, so it had to be in this book!

- 2 butternut squash, peeled, seeded and halved lengthwise
- ½ cup + 2 Tbsp (155 mL) extra virgin olive oil, divided
- Kosher salt
- Fresh black pepper
- 1 medium onion, diced
- 1 leek (white part only), sliced thin
- 1 shallot, sliced thin
- 1 Tbsp (15 mL) ginger, peeled and chopped
- 1 tsp (5 mL) curry powder
- ½ cup (125 mL) white wine
- 6 cups (1.5 L) vegetable stock (for homemade, see page 114)
- 1 cup (250 mL) coconut milk
- 1 sprig thyme
- 4–6 tsp (20–30 mL) roasted pumpkin seeds, for garnish
- 18 slices pickled ginger (recipe follows), for garnish
- 18 paper-thin red chili slices, for garnish
- 18 coriander cress stems, for garnish

Preheat oven to 175°C (350°F).

Place the squash (cut sides up) on a parchment-lined baking sheet. Fill the cavity of each squash half with 1 Tbsp (15 mL) olive oil and season with 1 tsp (5 mL) salt and ¼ tsp (1 mL) pepper. Roast the squash for about 1 hour and 20 minutes, until tender.

While the squash is cooking, heat ½ cup (125 mL) olive oil in a large soup pot over medium heat. Add the onion, leek, shallot, ginger and curry powder and cook until lightly browned. Add the wine and reduce completely.

Remove the squash from the oven, scoop out the flesh and discard the skin. Add the cooked squash, stock, coconut milk and thyme to the pot with the onions. Simmer over medium-low for 15 minutes, then remove the thyme.

Working in batches, purée the soup in a high-speed blender until smooth; season with salt and pepper to taste.

Pour the hot soup into bowls or soup plates. Sprinkle the pumpkin seeds over the soup. In the centre of each bowl of soup place a few pickled ginger slices, red chili slices and coriander cress stems. Enjoy while nice and hot.

PICKLED GINGER

- ½ cup (125 mL) thinly sliced ginger (skin scraped off)
- ⅓ cup (80 mL) rice vinegar
- ⅓ cup (80 mL) sugar
- ⅓ cup (80 mL) water
- 1 red Anaheim chili
- 1 pinch saffron

In a medium pot, add the ginger with enough water to cover. Bring to a boil, then quickly remove the ginger and shock in a bowl of ice water. Repeat this procedure two more times. Drain and place the blanched ginger in a medium bowl.

In a medium pot, add the vinegar, sugar, water, chili and saffron and bring to a boil over medium heat. Once boiling, remove from heat and pour over the blanched ginger until fully submerged. Let the mixture cool, then transfer the ginger with the pickling liquid to a sealed airtight container and place in the fridge for at least 30 minutes.

CUMIN *and* CARROT SOUP

MAKES 4–6 SERVINGS

- 3 Tbsp (45 mL) grapeseed oil
- 1 onion, finely diced
- 1 tsp (5 mL) ground cumin
- ¼ tsp (1 mL) turmeric
- 1 lb (450 g) carrots, peeled and diced
- 1 medium russet potato, peeled and cubed
- 2¼ cups (560 mL) vegetable stock (for homemade, see page 114)
- 1½ cups (375 mL) coconut milk + more as needed
- Kosher salt
- Fresh black pepper
- 1 pinch cayenne pepper, for garnish
- Extra virgin olive oil, for serving
- 20 cilantro leaves, for garnish

There's nothing more comforting than a big bowl of soup, and this recipe is as comforting as they come. Featuring a creamy coconut milk base and a few subtle spices, this vibrant orange soup is sure to have you feeling all warm and fuzzy inside!

Heat the grapeseed oil in a large pot over medium heat. Add the onion and cook until softened, then add the cumin and turmeric and cook for another couple minutes. Add the carrots and potato and cook for 5 minutes, stirring occasionally. Add the vegetable stock and coconut milk and bring to a simmer. Cover and let the mixture cook until all of the vegetables are tender, about 20 minutes.

In a high-speed blender, pulse the soup until smooth, then pass it through a fine mesh sieve to filter out any lumps. Tweak the seasoning with salt and pepper and adjust the consistency with more coconut milk if necessary.

Fill soup bowls two-thirds with soup and garnish with a bit of cayenne pepper, a dash of olive oil and some cilantro leaves.

CHILLED SWEET CORN SOUP

MAKES 4–6 SERVINGS

- 3 cups (750 mL) fresh corn kernels, divided
- 2 yellow heirloom tomatoes, cored and diced
- 1 yellow pepper, seeded and diced
- ¼ cup (60 mL) extra virgin olive oil + extra for serving
- ½ cucumber, peeled and chopped
- 2 Tbsp (30 mL) sherry vinegar
- Sea salt
- Fresh black pepper
- 12 cherry tomatoes, halved
- 12 cilantro leaves, for garnish
- 1 jalapeno, seeded and sliced, for garnish
- Maldon salt, for garnish

Add a little southern comfort to your afternoon with this bright and spicy corn gazpacho. Pair with a piece (or two) of cornbread and dig into this refreshing sunny summer-day meal!

In a high-speed blender, combine 2 cups (500 mL) corn kernels with the tomatoes, yellow pepper, cucumber, olive oil, sherry vinegar, 1 tsp (5 mL) sea salt and ¼ tsp (1 mL) pepper and blend until smooth. Pass through a fine mesh sieve into a large bowl and adjust the seasoning with salt and pepper to taste. Reserve in the fridge until cold.

Fill soup bowls two-thirds with very cold soup (I recommend using beautiful terra cotta bowls) and portion the remaining corn kerels and the cherry tomatoes into the centre of each bowl, surrounded by cilantro and jalapeno slices. Drizzle with olive oil and sprinkle with Maldon salt.

CLASSIC GAZPACHO

MAKES 4–6 SERVINGS

Soup is such a nostalgic comfort food, but in the summer months you probably aren't craving a piping hot meal. This tomato and cucumber gazpacho is a refreshing soup that's sure to keep you cool while you're lounging in the summer sun. And for a hot tip, I personally add a bit of Tabasco to add some kick.

---

2 lb (900 g) ripe Roma tomatoes, cored, seeded and diced

1 small cucumber, peeled, seeded and diced

1 red pepper, seeded and diced

½ onion, diced

2 cloves garlic

2 Tbsp (30 mL) sherry vinegar

1 tsp (5 mL) sea salt + more as needed

3 Tbsp (45 mL) extra virgin olive oil + 1 Tbsp (15 mL) for serving

½ tsp (2 mL) cracked black pepper

½ tsp (2 mL) ground cumin

1 thick slice of white bread, crust removed, diced

1 pinch Maldon salt, for garnish

1 Tbsp (15 mL) chopped fines herbes (parsley, chives and chervil), for garnish

2 cups (500 mL) garlic croutons (page 117), for garnish

Combine all the ingredients, except for the garnishes, in a food processor and mix on high for 1 minute or until the desired consistency is reached (it should be thick but pourable). Refrigerate in a covered pitcher or large bowl for at least 4 hours and adjust the seasoning with salt to taste.

Fill bowls two-thirds with soup and drizzle with olive oil, sprinkle with Maldon salt and garnish with fines herbes and croutons.

CURRIED COCONUT SQUASH STEW

MAKES 4–6 SERVINGS

½ cinnamon stick
2 star anise
2 Tbsp (30 mL) vegetable oil
¼ cup (60 mL) diced onion
5 cloves garlic, minced
¾ cup (185 mL) diced ginger (skin scraped off)
¾ cup (185 mL) peeled and diced galangal
2 stalks lemongrass, smashed
½ tsp (2 mL) ground coriander seeds
½ tsp (2 mL) ground cumin seeds
¼ tsp (1 mL) turmeric
1 bird's eye chili, seeded and sliced into thin rings
3 lime leaves
1 Tbsp (15 mL) yellow curry paste
2 cups (500 mL) coconut milk
1 Tbsp (15 mL) palm sugar (grated, if purchased in a solid form)
¼ cup (60 mL) lime juice
Kosher salt
1¼ lb (560 g) butternut squash
1 lb (450 g) acorn squash
1 lb (450 g) kabocha squash
1 lb (450 g) delicata squash
¼ cup (60 mL) extra virgin olive oil
2 Tbsp (30 mL) pickled ginger (page 121), for garnish
¼ cup (60 mL) roasted unsalted cashews, roughly chopped, for garnish
20 cilantro leaves, for garnish
20 red sorrel leaves, for garnish
2 cups (500 mL) fried kale chips (recipe follows), for garnish

This is the kind of dish that will take you on a vacation with its excellent balance of delicate and light flavours. It remains a popular dish among lovers of plant-based foods and even those who are harder to convince.

In a small dry pan, toast the cinnamon stick and star anise over medium heat until fragrant, about 1–2 minutes. Set aside.

Heat the vegetable oil in a large pot over medium heat. Sweat the onion, garlic, ginger and galangal. Add the lemongrass and stir. Add the toasted cinnamon and star anise as well as the coriander, cumin, turmeric, bird's eye chili, lime leaves and curry paste; cook until fragrant, about 5 minutes, stirring often. Add the coconut milk and bring to a simmer over medium-low heat. Cook for 30 minutes, then remove from heat and rest at room temperature, uncovered, for about 15–20 minutes while the flavours infuse.

In a separate medium pot, melt the palm sugar with the lime juice over medium-low heat, about 2–3 minutes, stirring often. Remove from heat, strain the infused curry sauce over the lime–palm sugar mixture and return to the stove over medium-low heat. Reduce to the desired consistency (it should coat the back of a spoon) and season with salt to taste. Set aside at room temperature.

Preheat oven to 175°C (350°F).

Peel and cut each squash in half, then slice each half into about 6 crescents. Use a peeler to shape the crescents into perfect half-moons, then toss them in a large bowl with ¼ cup (60 mL) olive oil and 1 Tbsp (15 mL) salt. Layer the squash on a parchment-lined baking tray and bake until cooked but still firm, about 8–10 minutes.

Divide the squash into 2 vacuum seal bags with 1 cup (250 mL) of the curry sauce per bag. Seal the bags and place in a circulator at 70°C (160°F) until the squash has finished cooking, about 15–20 minutes. (If you don't have a circulator, place the squash and in a large pot with enough curry sauce to cover it; cover the pot and cook over medium-low heat, so that the squash cooks really slowly while absorbing the flavours of the curry sauce, about 12–15 minutes.)

Once cooked, add the squash back to the remaining curry sauce (either strain out the liquid with a fine mesh sieve and discard to keep the sauce fresh, or add the liquid back to the curry sauce with the squash).

PICKLED GARNISHES Toast the peppercorns and coriander seeds in a small dry pan over medium heat until fragrant, about 1–2 minutes. Add the toasted spices to a medium saucepan and combine with the shallot, garlic, vinegar, water, caster sugar, bay leaf and thyme. Bring to a simmer over medium heat and cook for 5 minutes. Remove from heat and let the mixture steep until cooled, then pass through a sieve. Reserve the liquid and discard the remaining ingredients.

Peel off the first layer of the hearts of palm and slice the remaining layers really thinly into a small bowl with a mandoline. In a small saucepan, bring half the pickling liquid to a boil then pour it over the hearts of palm until submerged; let it cool to room temperature.

Cut a 3-inch (8 cm) chunk from the top of the butternut squash and, using a ring mold, cut a puck from the chunk. Thinly slice the puck using a mandoline and place it in a bowl. In a small saucepan, bring the remaining pickling liquid to a boil and pour it over the squash, then let it cool to room temperature.

SAUTÉED KALE Heat the olive oil in a medium pot over a medium-low heat. Add the kale until it begins to soften, then add the garlic and shallot; deglaze with lemon juice. Add salt and pepper to taste.

ASSEMBLY Place some curry sauce in the centre of a deep plate and top with a few curried squash crescents. Add the sautéed kale and more curried squash crescents on top. Add the pickled garnishes and ginger above and around the squash and sprinkle with the cashews. Finish with the cilantro and sorrel leaves and top with kale chips.

You're there, it smells amazing and now I'm jealous.

PICKLED GARNISHES

½ tsp (2 mL) peppercorns

½ tsp (2 mL) coriander seeds

½ shallot, diced

1 clove garlic, minced

1 cup (250 mL) champagne vinegar

⅔ cup (160 mL) water

⅔ cup (160 mL) caster sugar

1 bay leaf

2 sprigs thyme

⅔ cup (160 mL) fresh hearts of palm

3½ oz (100 g) butternut squash

SAUTÉED KALE

4 tsp (20 mL) extra virgin olive oil

1 bunch black kale, spines removed, leaves massaged and julienned

1 clove garlic, minced

½ shallot, sliced

½ lemon, juiced

Kosher salt

Fresh black pepper

FRIED KALE CHIPS

Wash the kale and pat dry; remove the stalks and tear the leaves into large pieces.

Fill a medium pot two-thirds full with vegetable oil and heat to 175°C (350°F). Fry the kale until crispy, about 15–30 seconds, at which point it will start to change colour (watch out for splatters). Remove the kale and place it on a paper towel to dry; season with salt to taste.

½ bunch green kale

Vegetable oil, for frying

Kosher salt

SWEET CORN *and* TOMATO CHILI

MAKES 4–6 SERVINGS

1 cup (250 mL) dry kidney beans, soaked overnight, drained and rinsed (see note)

6 sprigs thyme

4 whole cloves garlic + 3 minced cloves

6 cups (1.5 L) vegetable stock (for homemade, see page 114)

1 cup (250 mL) dry black beans, soaked overnight, drained and rinsed (see note)

2 Tbsp (30 mL) vegetable oil

One 28 oz (794 g) can peeled San Marzano tomatoes, diced

½ onion, diced

1 Tbsp (15 mL) chili powder

½ Tbsp (7 mL) smoked paprika

2 Tbsp (30 mL) cumin

⅛ tsp (0.5 mL) cayenne

¼ tsp (1 mL) sea salt

⅛ tsp (0.5 mL) cracked black pepper

3 Tbsp (45 mL) tomato paste

Kernels from 4 ears of corn

1 cup (250 mL) sliced green onions, for garnish

¼ cup (60 mL) cilantro, for garnish

1 cup (250 mL) Pebre (page 39), for serving

2 limes, cut into wedges, for serving

8–10 Corn Tortillas (page 48), for serving

There's nothing quite like the irresistible combination of heat and sweet. This sweet corn chili combined with pebre strikes the perfect balance between the two for a spicy dinner to savour with the family!

In a medium pot, combine the kidney beans, 3 sprigs thyme, 2 whole garlic cloves and 3 cups (750 mL) vegetable stock. In a second medium pot, combine the black beans with the remaining 3 sprigs thyme, 2 whole garlic cloves and 3 cups (750 mL) vegetable stock. Bring both pots to a boil and cook until tender, about 10–15 minutes. Remove from heat and cool; discard the thyme and garlic cloves. Drain the beans but reserve the liquid from the black beans.

Heat the vegetable oil in a large Dutch oven over medium heat and sauté the 3 minced garlic cloves and diced onion until translucent and starting to brown. Add the chili powder, paprika, cumin, cayenne, salt and pepper and stir for a minute or two, until well combined. Add the tomato paste, beans (and black bean liquid, if using cooked beans) and corn to the onions and cook over low heat, covered, for 4–5 hours, stirring often.

Serve the chili in beautiful tera cotta dishes if you have them, although any coupe plates or bowls will do. (Alternatively, you can serve the chili family-style in a large dish.) Add the chopped green onions overtop with some cilantro leaves. Serve the pebre on the side with lime wedges and tortillas.

NOTE: If you prefer to use canned beans, double the volume (2 cups/ 500 mL instead of 1 cup/250 mL) and omit the thyme, whole garlic cloves and vegetable stock. Skip the first paragraph of the method—you can add the drained and rinsed beans directly to the onion mixture.

MAINS

CANNELLINI BEAN POT PIE

MAKES ONE 5-INCH (12 CM) PIE

½ cup (125 mL) dry cannelloni beans, soaked overnight, drained and rinsed (see note)

4 cups (1 L) vegetable stock, divided (for homemade, see page 114)

2 Tbsp (30 mL) olive oil + enough to cover the bottom of a skillet and as needed

½ shallot, finely diced

Kosher salt

¼ lb (115 g) sweet potato, peeled and cubed

¼ lb (115 g) Yukon gold potato, peeled and cubed

¼ onion, finely diced

¼ red pepper, seeded and diced

¼ lb (115 g) portobello mushrooms, sliced

½ tsp (2 mL) smoked paprika

1 tsp (5 mL) garlic powder

3 stalks thyme, leaves picked and chopped

1 Tbsp (15 mL) all-purpose flour

½ Tbsp (7 mL) soy sauce

1 recipe savoury pie dough (recipe follows)

This vegan pot pie is filled with natural sugar, spice and everything nice. The wholesome vegetables and creamy beans meld together into a comforting family dinner to share around the table. Accompany with the Green Bean Salad with Champagne Dressing (page 111).

Add the beans to a medium pot with 3 cups (750 mL) vegetable stock and cook over medium heat until tender, about 15–20 minutes. Strain through a sieve.

In a medium skillet over medium-high heat, add enough olive oil to cover the bottom of the skillet. Add the shallot and beans to the skillet and let them cook without stirring for few minutes to crisp them up, then stir and cook for another 5 minutes. Season with ½ tsp (2 mL) salt.

In a large skillet, heat 2 Tbsp (30 mL) olive oil over medium-high heat and add the sweet potato, Yukon potato, onion, red pepper and mushrooms. Cook uncovered, stirring occasionally, until the potatoes are tender, then reduce heat to low. Add the paprika, garlic powder, thyme and flour and stir until the vegetables are coated. Add 1 cup (250 mL) vegetable stock and soy sauce and stir for about 5 minutes, until the mix thickens up. Add the crispy beans and shallots and adjust the seasoning with salt to taste. Pour the bean filling into a 5-inch (12 cm) deep dish pan.

ASSEMBLY Preheat oven to 230°C (450°F).

Remove the pie dough from the fridge and let it come slightly to temperature (about 5–10 minutes), then roll it out on a floured surface until large enough to cover the pie dish. Drape the dough over the pan and trim any excess pastry. Lightly crimp up the edges and cut 4 slits into the centre to vent out the steam. Brush some olive oil on top of the dough.

Bake for about 25 minutes or until the pastry is golden and crispy. Remove the pie from the oven and let it rest for a bit before cutting into slices and serving on flat plates.

NOTE: If you prefer, you can substitute the dry beans with 1¼ cups (310 mL) canned. If using canned, omit the vegetable stock and skip straight to the second paragraph of the method—you can add the drained and rinsed beans directly to the skillet.

SAVOURY PIE DOUGH

In a medium bowl, combine the flour, salt, baking powder and sage. Add the coconut oil and mix until you obtain a coarse meal texture. Form a well in the centre of the flour mixture and add the water; mix until you are able to form a ball. Knead until the dough isn't sticking to your hands, then wrap it in plastic and let it rest for a minimum of 30 minutes in the fridge.

⅔ cup (160 mL) all-purpose flour

¼ tsp (1 mL) kosher salt

⅛ tsp (0.5 mL) baking powder

1 stalk sage, leaves picked and chopped

¼ cup (60 mL) refined coconut oil (room temperature), cut into small cubes

3½ Tbsp (52 mL) ice cold water

RATATOUILLE-STUFFED MUSHROOMS

MAKES 4 SERVINGS

6 Tbsp (90 mL) olive oil, divided

⅔ red onion, brunoised

2 cloves garlic, minced + 2 whole cloves

1 red pepper, seeded and diced

1 medium eggplant, diced

1 zucchini, diced small

2 plum tomatoes, peeled, cored and diced small

2 stalks oregano, leaves picked and chopped

Kosher salt

Fresh black pepper

1 lemon, juiced and zested

4 giant portobello mushrooms, top skin peeled using your fingers

¼ cup (60 mL) almond pesto (page 157)

4 basil leaves

Mushrooms are the perfect vessel for this comforting classic ratatouille recipe. This earthy, meaty, hearty dish is sure to be the main event at a summer evening dinner. Serve with an exquisite side salad for the full effect, such as the Green Salad with Lemon Dressing (page 93).

Preheat oven to 200°C (400°F).

In a large, deep pan, heat 2 Tbsp (30 mL) olive oil over medium heat. Add the onion and sweat without browning, stirring occasionally, until translucent. Add the minced garlic and cook until fragrant. Add the red pepper and sauté. Repeat the process with the eggplant and zucchini. Stir occasionally, then add the tomatoes, oregano and 1 tsp (5 mL) salt and ¼ tsp (1 mL) black pepper. Cook for 2–3 minutes, ensuring all the vegetables retain some crunch and texture. Finish with the lemon juice and zest. If too watery, cook until the water evaporates.

Place the mushrooms on a parchment-lined baking tray and grate half a garlic clove over each. Drizzle 1 Tbsp (15 mL) olive oil over each mushroom along with ¼ tsp (1 mL) salt and a crack of black pepper. Bake for 10–12 minutes, until the mushrooms are cooked and softened.

Stuff the mushrooms with the ratatouille and place back in the oven for 5 minutes or until nice and hot. Remove from the oven and sprinkle with salt to taste; garnish with almond pesto and basil leaves. Place each portobello mushroom in the middle of a plate and pair with a salad.

CAULIFLOWER TIKKA MASALA

MAKES 4–6 SERVINGS

Take your taste buds on a trip across the globe and indulge in this complex spice profile famous in Indian cuisine. The spices meld together to create a comforting and warming dish that's best served with friends, family and a side of pita or naan.

- 1 Tbsp (15 mL) vegetable oil, divided
- 1 onion, diced
- 2 oz (60 g) ginger, peeled and brunoised
- 6 cloves garlic, minced
- 1 bird's eye chili
- Kosher salt
- 1 tsp (5 mL) turmeric
- ½ tsp (2 mL) cayenne pepper
- ½ Tbsp (7 mL) smoked paprika, divided
- ½ Tbsp (7 mL) ground coriander, divided
- ½ Tbsp (7 mL) garam masala, divided
- 2 tsp (10 mL) dried fenugreek leaves
- ½ red pepper, seeded and diced
- One 28 oz (794 g) can peeled San Marzano tomatoes, diced
- ¼ cup (60 mL) coconut yogurt (full fat) + more as needed
- 1 lemon, zested
- Maple syrup, as needed
- 1 head cauliflower, broken down to florets
- 1 tsp (5 mL) lemon juice
- ½ tsp (2 mL) ground cumin
- ½ tsp (2 mL) garlic powder
- ¼ cup (60 mL) cilantro, for garnish
- 12 fenugreek leaves, for garnish

Heat a large Dutch oven over medium-high heat and, once hot, add 1 tsp (5 mL) vegetable oil. Add the diced onion, ginger, garlic and bird's eye chili and cook until the mixture begins to sweat. Add a good pinch of salt and mix well. Cook, stirring occasionally, until the onions are translucent.

Add the turmeric, cayenne, 1 tsp (5 mL) smoked paprika, 1 tsp (5 mL) coriander, 1 tsp (5 mL) garam masala and the fenugreek leaves; cook for 1 minute, until fragrant. Add the diced red pepper, tomatoes (with their juices) and coconut yogurt. Season again with 2 tsp (10 mL) salt. Reduce to a really low simmer and cook for about 45 minutes, stirring often.

Adjust the seasoning with salt and pepper to taste, add the lemon zest and add maple syrup for sweetness, if needed. Let it cool as the aromas settle.

Preheat oven to 200°C (400°F).

In a large bowl, mix the cauliflower florets with the lemon juice and remaining 2 tsp (10 mL) vegetable oil. Combine the cumin, garlic powder, ½ tsp (2 mL) smoked paprika, ½ tsp (2 mL) coriander, ½ tsp (2 mL) garam masala and 2 tsp (10 mL) salt and sprinkle over the cauliflower; stir until coated. Spread the cauliflower florets on a parchment-lined baking sheet and bake for 20 minutes.

Remove the cauliflower from the oven and, in a large pot, combine the baked florets with the tikka masala. You can add more coconut yogurt if desired. Mix well and bring to a simmer over low heat. Add salt, if needed.

In a large, beautiful dish, plate the tikka masala. Garnish with cilantro and fenugreek leaves.

GREEN FALAFEL

MAKES 4 SERVINGS

Falafel is a Mediterranean, chickpea-based patty that is rich in refreshing spices and packed with plant-based protein. The herbaceous patties pair perfectly with a drizzle of my nutty and creamy Tahini Dip (page 36). Serve with a squeeze of lemon for an elegant and complete main course meal.

2 cups (500 mL) dry chickpeas, soaked overnight, drained and rinsed (see note)

6 cups (1.5 L) vegetable stock (for homemade, see page 114)

Kosher salt

½ red onion, diced

2 cloves garlic, minced

1 serrano pepper, seeded and diced

½ cup (125 mL) parsley leaves

½ cup (125 mL) cilantro leaves

½ cup (125 mL) all-purpose flour

1 lemon, zested

1 Tbsp (15 mL) lemon juice

1 Tbsp (15 mL) ground cumin

1 Tbsp (15 mL) ground coriander

½ tsp (2 mL) baking soda

Vegetable oil, for frying

1 lemon, cut into wedges, for serving

5 stalks cilantro, leaves picked, for garnish

Tahini Dip (page 36), for serving

In a medium-to-large pot, add the chickpeas and vegetable stock and cook over medium heat until soft and fully cooked, about 18–20 minutes. Season with 2 tsp (10 mL) salt and remove from heat. Cool completely in the liquid, then drain.

Add the onion, garlic, serrano pepper, parsley and cilantro to a food processor and blend on high speed until everything is finely minced. Stop and scrape down the sides of the machine.

Add the drained chickpeas to the onion mixture in the food processor and pulse until they start to break down. Scrape down the sides then add the flour, lemon zest and juice, cumin, coriander, 1 tsp (5 mL) salt and baking soda and process until the mixture is even and finely ground (not pasty). It should hold together if you squeeze it between your fingers. Adjust seasoning with salt if needed.

Using a 1½-inch (4 cm) scoop, scoop out the chickpea mixture and roll it between the palms of your hands (you should aim for a perfectly round ball). Reserve the falafel on a tray until all the mix is used up.

Fill a large pot with at least 3 inches (8 cm) of vegetable oil and heat until the oil reaches 175°C (350°F). Using a slotted spoon, carefully drop the falafel balls into the oil. Work in batches so that you don't overcrowd the pan (you don't want the temperature of the oil to drop too much) and fry until deep brown, about 3–4 minutes. Remove one ball and open it with a fork to ensure that it's fully cooked, then place the falafel on a paper towel to absorb the excess grease. Season with salt to taste.

Pile the falafel nicely in a large deep plate. Serve with lemon wedges on the side and garnish with cilantro leaves overtop. Serve the Tahini Dip in a small jar or ramekin on the side.

NOTE: If you prefer, you can substitute the dry chickpeas with 6 cups (1.5 L) canned. If using canned, omit the vegetable stock and skip straight to the second paragraph of the method—you can add the drained and rinsed chickpeas directly to the onion mixture.

TEMPURA MUSHROOM MAKI ROLL

MAKES 6 ROLLS

1 cup (250 mL) sushi rice, rinsed until the water runs through clear

1½ cups (375 mL) water

2 Tbsp (30 mL) sugar

¼ cup (60 mL) rice vinegar

Kosher salt

6 roasted nori sheets

1 Tbsp (15 mL) pickled ginger (page 121)

½ cup (125 mL) julienned scallions (green part only)

¼ cup (60 mL) coriander cress (or cilantro leaves) + extra for garnish

¼ cup (60 mL) red shiso cress (or regular chopped shiso) + extra for garnish

Olive oil, for frying

1 red chili, seeded and sliced thin

¼ cup (60 mL) Miso Mayo (page 38)

MUSHROOM FILLING

2 Tbsp (30 mL) vegetable oil

1 lb (450 g) white mushrooms, quartered

1 Tbsp (15 mL) ginger, brunoised

2 cloves garlic, minced

1 Tbsp (15 mL) soy sauce

1 Tbsp (15 mL) yuzu sauce

Kosher salt

TEMPURA BATTER

1 cup (250 mL) all-purpose flour

1 cup (250 mL) rice flour

1 cup (250 mL) corn starch

¼ cup (60 mL) baking powder

6 cups (1.5 L) sparkling water

Sushi dates are always in season, and tempura is a must-have addition to any maki roll! Impress your loved ones with a plant-based sushi experience that features all of the iconic flavours you want, as well as the crunchy bites you crave.

Add the rice and water to a medium pot over medium-high heat and heat to a simmer, stirring occasionally. Once the water begins to boil, turn the heat all the way down to a light simmer, cover the pot and cook for 6–8 minutes. Check that the water is completely absorbed and the rice is cooked.

Place the rice in a large mixing bowl. Add the sugar, vinegar and ½ tsp (2 mL) salt and stir to combine. Spread the rice on a parchment-lined baking sheet, fanning the rice to make it cool as fast as possible. Once cool, move the rice into a container and cover with plastic wrap. Set aside at room temperature.

MUSHROOM FILLING In a large skillet, heat 2 Tbsp (30 mL) vegetable oil over medium-high heat. Add the mushrooms and sear, making sure not to overcrowd the skillet (work in batches if you need to—if you overcrowd, the mushrooms won't sear properly and will release too much water).

Add the ginger and garlic and cook for 2 minutes. Deglaze with the soy and yuzu sauces. Adjust the seasoning with salt to taste and remove from heat. Let the mushrooms cool.

TEMPURA BATTER In a large bowl, mix all the dry ingredients together. (Please note that you will have more dry mix than needed to complete the recipe.) In a stainless steel bowl, combine ½ cup (125 mL) of the dry mix with sparkling water until the mix begins to resemble waffle batter. It should be thick enough to coat the maki rolls; you can add more sparkling water to thin it out if necessary. (You may wish to make extra batter in case you need a bit more.)

ASSEMBLY Wrap the sushi mat in plastic wrap (it'll help prolong the life of the mat). Lay the first nori sheet on top of the mat, wet your hands and cover three-quarters of the nori sheet with a thin layer of rice.

Place the mushrooms on top of the rice in a 2-inch (5 cm) thick line. On top of the mushrooms, add some pickled ginger, scallion curls and cresses. Brush water on the part of the nori sheet without rice and roll the maki tightly over itself until firmly sealed. Repeat the steps to make additional maki rolls.

Fill a Dutch oven halfway with vegetable oil and heat until the oil reaches 160°C (325°F). Dip each maki roll in the tempura batter, making sure it's well coated and shaking any excess if necessary. Place into the oil and fry until crispy, about 2–3 minutes. Remove with a slotted spoon.

Place the maki rolls on paper towels to absorb any excess oil then sprinkle with salt. Slice the rolls into 2-inch (5 cm) thick coils and place on a long rectangular dish. Garnish each coil with chili rounds, Miso Mayo, cilantro and shiso cress.

Chef Matt Ravenscroft
CULINARY DIRECTOR, GIA

SWEET POTATO GRATIN

MAKES 4–6 SERVINGS

Sweet potato medallions make up the base of this decadent, creamy dish. The gratin features a unique burst of sweetness and a thick, rich texture that's sure to please all vegetable naysayers at the table! Serve with a Green Salad with Lemon Dressing (page 93) for the perfect burst of sweet and citrusy flavours.

- 2 tsp (10 mL) vegetable oil + extra for the dish
- ½ onion, julienned
- 1 clove garlic, minced
- ¼ tsp (1 mL) ground cinnamon
- Kosher salt
- Fresh black pepper
- 3 Tbsp (45 mL) raw unsalted cashews, soaked overnight and drained
- 3½ Tbsp (52 mL) nutritional yeast
- ½ cup (125 mL) unsweetened coconut milk
- 3 sweet potatoes, peeled and sliced paper thin with a mandoline
- ⅔ cup (160 mL) unsweetened soy milk
- 4 stalks oregano, leaves picked and chopped
- Green Salad with Lemon Dressing (page 93), for serving

Preheat oven to 200°C (400°F).

In a medium pan, heat the vegetable oil over medium heat. Add the onion and garlic and sauté until translucent and fragrant. Remove from heat, stir in the cinnamon and season with 1 tsp (5 mL) salt and ¼ tsp (1 mL) black pepper. Set aside.

Add the cashews to a high-speed blender with the nutritional yeast and coconut milk. Blend until smooth and creamy.

To build the gratin, spray or brush oil onto a 9- × 13-inch (23 × 33 cm) ovenproof dish. Start layering with a bit of the blended cashew cream, then add the sweet potatoes (overlapping in the same direction), onion mixture and more cashew cream. Repeat until you've used all the sweet potatoes, seasoning with ¼ tsp (2 mL) salt and a couple twists of a pepper mill every couple layers.

In a large stainless steel bowl, combine the remaining cashew cream with the soy milk, chopped oregano and salt to taste. Pour the mix over the gratin.

Cook in the oven for about 35 minutes, then switch the oven to broil for about 2 minutes to get a nice crispy top.

Cut up the gratin into slices of whatever size you prefer. Place a slice of sweet potato gratin onto each plate with a good amount of salad next to it.

DEEP-FRIED TOMATILLO TACOS

MAKES 8–10 TACOS

4 large tomatillos, peeled and sliced

½ cup (125 mL) all-purpose flour

⅛ tsp (0.5 mL) cayenne

¼ tsp (1 mL) fresh black pepper

Kosher salt

1 cup (250 mL) coconut yogurt

2 cups (500 mL) breadcrumbs

Vegetable oil, for frying

Eight to ten 5-inch (12 cm) Corn Tortillas (page 48), warmed*

Creamy Avocado Dip (page 34), for serving

Tomato and Serrano Salsa (page 35), for serving

¼ cup (60 mL) cilantro leaves, for garnish

2 limes, quartered, for serving

---

*To heat the tortillas, place them on a baking tray and warm in a 175°C (350°F) oven for 2–3 minutes.

I never had a tomatillo until I moved to Canada. One day my friend Andres made fried tomatillos for our staff meal and I have been obsessed ever since. Here is a good recipe that I love to make on taco Tuesdays or . . . any day, really. Who's to say when is a good time to eat these delicious beauties!

Remove the papery husks from the tomatillos and discard; rinse them clean and pat dry (tomatillos sometimes have a really sticky coat to them). Cut the tomatillos into ½-inch (1 cm) thick slices.

In a medium bowl, combine the flour, cayenne, pepper and ½ tsp (2 mL) salt and cayenne. In a second bowl, add the coconut yogurt; fill a third bowl with the breadcrumbs. Dredge one tomatillo slice at a time in the flour. Shake off any excess, then submerge into the coconut yogurt to coat. Lift it out of the yogurt with your other hand (the idea is to keep one hand dry at all times) and let any excess drip off. Finally, coat the tomatillo in breadcrumbs, using your dry hand to pat the coating all over before lifting it out. Set the breaded tomatillos on a tray or large plate and repeat with the remaining slices.

In a wide, heavy pan, heat about ½ inch (1 cm) oil over medium-high heat until the oil reaches about 185°C (375°F). Once the oil is hot, fry as many coated tomatillo slices as you can fit in a single layer without crowding or touching one another in the pan. Fry until golden brown, flipping them so that both sides are evenly fried.

Remove each slice with a fork or tong and place on a cooling rack over paper towels or a baking sheet to catch any excess oil. Sprinkle with salt and repeat with the remaining slices.

You can either serve this dish DIY and let everyone make their own tacos, or you can assemble them ahead of serving. For the former, serve the tomatillo slices on a plate, the toppings in small bowls and the warmed up tortillas on the side. To assemble, start by adding some avocado cream to each taco shell, then add the tomatillo. Garnish with salsa and add some fresh cilantro on top with a lime wedge on the side.

FRIED TOFU *with* SWEET CHILI SAUCE

MAKES 4 SERVINGS

Crunchy, crispy tofu balanced with fresh acidic slaw. This is another dish I have served at my restaurants over the years, and the flavours and textures will dance in your mouth.

FRIED TOFU

Vegetable oil, for frying

⅓ cup (80 mL) rice flour

⅓ cup (80 mL) corn starch

Two 700 g blocks firm tofu, cut into 12 equal-sized rectangles

Kosher salt

SWEET CHILI SAUCE

2 Tbsp (30 mL) vegetable oil

4 Anaheim chilies, seeded and sliced

½ lb (450 g) Roma tomatoes, cored, seeded and diced

½ lb (450 g) red peppers, seeded and diced

1 cup (250 mL) water

1 cup (250 mL) champagne vinegar

½ cup (125 mL) sugar

Kosher salt

PEANUT BRITTLE

½ cup (125 mL) sugar

½ cup (125 mL) isomalt (or granulated sugar)

1 cup (250 mL) roasted peanuts, deshelled

GRILLED SCALLIONS

12 scallions

3 Tbsp (45 mL) olive oil

1 tsp (5 mL) kosher salt

FRIED TOFU Fill a large pot one-quarter full with vegetable oil and heat to 175°C (350°F). Mix the flour and corn starch together in a small bowl and dredge the tofu. Fry the tofu until golden brown and crispy, about 3–4 minutes.

Remove the tofu using a spider or large slotted spoon and place on absorbent paper to suck up any excess oil. Season with salt right away.

SWEET CHILI SAUCE In a medium pot, heat 2 Tbsp (30 mL) vegetable oil over medium heat. Add the chilies, tomatoes and peppers and lightly sweat, then add the water, vinegar and sugar. Bring to a simmer over medium-low heat and cook until the desired consistency is reached (it should be thick and sticky but pourable). Let the mixture cool, then blend in a food processor until smooth. Pass the mixture through a fine mesh sieve and adjust the seasoning with salt to taste. Store in a sealed airtight container in the fridge until needed.

PEANUT BRITTLE In a medium pot, combine the sugar and isomalt over high heat. Without stirring, heat until the sugar melts, begins to boil and turns into a caramel, about 5–6 minutes. Add the roasted peanuts and stir vigorously, then pour out the coated peanuts and caramel onto a parchment-lined baking sheet. Cool completely, then add to a food processor and blend on high speed until you obtain a coarse brittle.

GRILLED SCALLIONS In a medium bowl, toss the scallions with 3 Tbsp (45 mL) olive oil and 1 tsp (5 mL) salt. Grill the scallions on a barbecue or in a cast iron pan over high heat, flipping sides halfway through, until charred and soft, about 3–4 minutes.

ASSEMBLY Place the fried tofu in the centre of a plate and top with pickled slaw. Add a spoonful of brittle on one side of the tofu and the grilled spring onions around the opposite side. Finish by generously drizzling sweet chili sauce around the plate and top with coriander leaves or cress.

GARNISHES

Pickled slaw (recipe follows)

¼ cup (60 mL) coriander cress (or regular cilantro leaves)

PICKLED SLAW

1½ cups (375 mL) sugar, divided

1 cup (250 mL) water, divided

2 star anise, divided

1 tsp (5 mL) coriander seeds

1 cup (250 mL) champagne vinegar

1 tsp (5 mL) fennel seeds

1 cup (250 mL) red wine vinegar

¾ cup (185 mL) red onion, julienned

1 cup (250 mL) red cabbage, julienned

1 cup (250 mL) carrots, peeled and julienned

1 cup (250 mL) white cabbage, julienned

In a medium pot, combine half the sugar, half the water and 1 star anise with the coriander seeds and champagne vinegar. In a second medium pot, add the remaining sugar, water and star anise with the fennel seeds and red wine vinegar. Bring both pots to a simmer over medium heat and cook for 5 minutes. Remove pots from heat and let the mixtures steep for another 10 minutes. Pass each pickling liquid through a fine mesh sieve into separate containers and set aside.

While still warm, pour the red wine vinegar pickling liquid into 2 medium bowls; submerge the red onions in one bowl and the red cabbage in the other. Pour the champagne vinegar pickling liquid into 2 more medium bowls; submerge the carrots in one and the white cabbage in the other.

Once cooled, transfer the vegetables with their pickling liquids into sealed airtight containers and place in the fridge for at least 30 minutes. When ready to serve, strain the pickling liquids and stir all the vegetables together to make a slaw.

FRIED EGGPLANT *with* TOMATO CONFIT *and* QUINOA

MAKES 4 SERVINGS

This recipe brings warmth and comfort to mind, and it's one of my favourites to enjoy when I feel like I need a little pick-me-up. Remember that food is healing.

QUINOA

- 6 peppercorns
- 2 bay leaves
- 3 sprigs thyme
- 1 shallot, roughly chopped
- ½ onion, roughly chopped
- 1 cup (250 mL) uncooked white quinoa
- 6 cups (1.5 L) fortified vegetable stock (see note page 114)
- 1 tsp (5 mL) kosher salt

TOMATO CONFIT

- 3 Roma tomatoes, cored, cut into quarters and seeded
- ½ cup (125 mL) olive oil
- 2 sprigs rosemary
- 3 sprigs thyme
- 1 tsp (5 mL) kosher salt

FRIED CAPERS

- Vegetable oil, for frying
- ¼ cup (60 mL) capers
- Kosher salt

FRIED EGGPLANT

- 4 medium Japanese eggplants
- Vegetable oil, for frying
- Kosher salt

. . . ingredients continued

QUINOA Make a sachet using cheesecloth and fill it with the peppercorns, bay leaves, thyme, shallot and onion; tie shut with kitchen twine.

In a medium pot, add the quinoa, vegetable stock, salt and sachet. Cook uncovered over medium-high heat for 10–12 minutes, or until tender; the stock should be completely absorbed, but you can add more if you like your quinoa very soft.

Remove from heat and cool the quinoa to room temperature by spreading it on a parchment-lined baking sheet.

TOMATO CONFIT In a large pot, add all the tomato confit ingredients and bring to a mild simmer over low heat. Cook until the tomatoes are soft, about 12–15 minutes. Remove from heat and let the mixture steep until the tomatoes have cooled completely in the pot.

FRIED CAPERS Fill a small pot halfway with vegetable oil over medium heat. Fry the capers until crispy, about 1 minute, then remove with a slotted spoon and place on a paper towel. Season with salt and set aside.

FRIED EGGPLANT Prick the eggplants with a skewer. Fill a large deep pan one-quarter full with vegetable oil and heat over medium-high, then fry the eggplants whole until soft. Using tongs, remove the eggplants and place them on a plate or baking tray; pat dry with a paper towel and season with salt.

. . . recipe continued

ASSEMBLY

3–4 Tbsp (45–60 mL) vegetable oil

4 cups (1 L) mustard greens

Kosher salt

Fresh black pepper

2 cups (500 mL) basil tomato sauce (recipe follows)

¼ cup (60 mL) sliced Kalamata olives

1 cup (250 mL) Pebre (page 39)

ASSEMBLY In a large frying pan, heat 3–4 Tbsp (45–60 mL) vegetable oil over medium-high heat. Add the mustard greens and cook until wilted, about 2–3 minutes. Season with salt and pepper to taste and dry on a paper towel.

In a medium pot, warm the tomato sauce over medium-high heat until nice and hot. Spread it in the centre of a coupe plate and spoon the quinoa overtop in a pile. Cut each eggplant into 3 equal pieces on the bias and place them around the quinoa. In between pieces of eggplant, add 3 tomato confit pieces per plate. On top of the quinoa, add some sautéed mustard green leaves, sliced olives and fried capers. Finish with the Pebre. Alternatively, you can serve everything together in a large family-style dish.

BASIL TOMATO SAUCE

1 Tbsp (15 mL) olive oil

¼ onion, finely diced

3 cloves garlic, finely diced

1 Tbsp (15 mL) tomato paste

Two 28 oz (794 mL) cans peeled San Marzano tomatoes

6 large fresh basil leaves

1 lemon, juiced

Kosher salt

In a large pot, heat the olive oil over medium-low heat. Add the onion and garlic, then stir and sweat without browning. Reduce heat to low and add the tomato paste. Stir and cook for another 2–3 minutes.

Pulse the tomatoes in a high-speed blender until you achieve a rough purée, then add this to the pot. Increase heat back to medium-low and cook for about 25 minutes, stirring occasionally, then add the fresh basil. Cook for another 15 minutes.

Add the lemon juice, season with salt to taste and stir. Place the sauce in a container to cool, then seal and place in the fridge for up to 3–5 days. Tomato sauce can also be frozen for a later use.

STUFFED ARTICHOKES *with* CAPONATA

MAKES 4 SERVINGS

4 globe artichokes
4 lemons, divided
6 cups (1.5 mL) water
Fresh black pepper
Kosher salt
¼ cup (60 mL) all-purpose flour
2 Tbsp (30 mL) extra virgin olive oil
Fleur de sel
20 tarragon leaves, for garnish

CAPONATA

¼ cup (60 mL) extra virgin olive oil, divided + more as needed
½ large onion, finely diced
2 cloves garlic, minced
Kosher salt
1 large eggplant, medium dice
1 red pepper, seeded and diced
1 Tbsp (15 mL) brown sugar
1½ cups (375 mL) Roma tomatoes, cored, seeded and diced
1½ Tbsp (22 mL) sherry vinegar
2 Tbsp (30 mL) capers
2 Tbsp (30 mL) Kalamata olives, pitted and sliced
¼ lemon, juiced (optional)

This dish was inspired by my summers spent in the south of France and Italy on the Mediterranean coast. They say that food tastes like the sunlight that helped it grow, and I truly felt that to be true in those days where warm weather went hand in hand with delicious fresh vegetables. Those experiences were the inspiration behind this recipe, which is one of my forever favourites and I hope it will be one of yours too.

Start by rotating an artichoke in your hand, breaking off the tail and removing the outside and any other hard leaves. Continue to turn the artichoke and, using a parrot or paring knife, remove the tough green skins. Take a lemon and rub the surface of the artichoke to avoid oxidation. Repeat with the remaining artichokes (you'll only need 1 lemon).

Juice 2 lemons and place the lemon juice, water, ¼ tsp (1 mL) black pepper and 2 tsp (10 mL) salt into a large pot. Bring to a simmer over medium-high heat, then whisk in the flour until fully combined. Add the artichokes and cover the pot with a cartouche made from parchment paper (cut it to the size of the pot and keep it flush with the edges). Cook until tender, about 10–12 minutes, then remove from heat. Transfer the artichokes and sauce to a medium dish, cover and cool in the fridge.

After they're cooked, remove the hair (aka the choke) from the centre of each artichoke with a spoon, leaving only the hearts exposed. Store in a small bowl until ready to serve.

CAPONATA In a large pot, warm 2 Tbsp (30 mL) olive oil over medium-high heat. Add the onion and sweat until translucent; add the garlic and cook for 2 minutes, then season with salt to taste. Add another 2 Tbsp (30 mL) olive oil and cook the diced eggplant until caramelized, stirring occasionally; season again with salt to taste. (Eggplants absorb olive oil quickly, so add more oil if the pan becomes dry to prevent the eggplant from burning.) Add the red pepper and cook for 3 minutes, then add the brown sugar and tomatoes and stir to combine. Cook for 2 minutes then deglaze with vinegar.

Reduce heat to low, add the capers and olives and cook for 15–20 minutes, stirring occasionally. Adjust the seasoning with salt to taste and add lemon juice if you want to make the dish a bit sharper.

ASSEMBLY In a large frying pan, heat 2 Tbsp (30 mL) olive oil over medium-high heat and sear the bottoms of the artichoke hearts for 2 minutes. Remove the hearts and place them on absorbent paper to soak up any excess oil.

Serve the artichokes in terra cotta plates. Place 1 artichoke in the centre of each plate and garnish with caponata topped with fleur de sel and 5 tarragon leaves per bowl. Cut the remaining lemon into wedges and serve on the side.

EGGPLANT *and* CHESTNUT MOUSSAKA

MAKES 4–6 SERVINGS

4 oz (120 g) firm tofu

2 large eggplants, sliced into ¼-inch (0.5 cm) thick rounds

6 Tbsp (90 mL) olive oil, divided

Kosher salt

7 oz (200 g) green lentils (about half a 15 oz/425 g can)

4 oz (120 mL) white mushrooms, finely chopped

½ cup (125 mL) water chestnuts, finely chopped

½ onion, finely chopped

1 stalk celery, finely chopped

1 medium red pepper, seeded and finely chopped

1 clove garlic, minced

½ tsp (2 mL) paprika

2 stalks fresh oregano, finely chopped

½ tsp (2 mL) cumin

1 stalk rosemary, finely chopped

⅛ tsp (0.5 mL) ground cinnamon

¼ cup (60 mL) tomato paste

½ cup (125 mL) basil tomato sauce (for homemade, see page 148)

½ Tbsp (7 mL) dark soy sauce

½ Tbsp (7 mL) brown sugar

Fresh black pepper

Layers of plant-based protein, complex flavours, a rich and creamy sauce and roasted rounds of eggplant combine to create this stunning Mediterranean-inspired dish. Serve with a beautiful salad at your next family gathering for a comforting and hearty dish that is sure to please all of your family's picky palates!

Preheat oven to 175°C (350°F).

Press the tofu to remove as much moisture as possible; you can do so by putting the tofu between 2 plates and adding weight. Press for about 30 minutes to an hour.

Brush the eggplant rounds with olive oil (you'll need about ¼ cup/ 60 mL) and season lightly with salt. Place onto parchment paper–lined baking trays and bake for 25 minutes, flipping once at the halfway mark. (Alternatively, you can grill the eggplant on a barbecue.) Once cooked, set the eggplant aside on the baking trays to cool at room temperature. Leave the oven on.

In a large bowl, mash the tofu with a fork and add the lentils, mushrooms and water chestnuts; stir to combine.

In a large, thick-bottomed dish, warm 2 Tbsp (30 mL) olive oil over medium-high heat. Add the onion, celery and red pepper and sweat for 4–5 minutes. Add some minced garlic, paprika, oregano, cumin, rosemary and cinnamon and give it a stir, then add the tofu mix to the pan and keep cooking over low heat for 15–20 minutes.

Add the tomato paste, tomato sauce and soy sauce; continue cooking for about 8 minutes, or until all the excess liquid is cooked off and you have a delicious soft mince mixture. Add in the brown sugar and season with salt and pepper.

BECHAMEL In a medium pot, bring the soy milk, garlic, bay leaf, shallot and nutmeg to a simmer over medium heat; reduce heat to low and let the mixture steep for few minutes. Strain into a bowl with a sieve and set aside.

In a small pot over medium-high heat, whisk the olive oil and flour together to make a roux; continue whisking until the roux is fully combined and the raw flour has been cooked out, about 2–3 minutes. Add the milk mixture to the roux, a little at a time, whisking vigorously. Continue to cook until you obtain a thick, shiny, velvety mix. Season with salt and pepper to taste.

ASSEMBLY Place half the eggplant rounds along the bottom of a 4- × 8-inch (10 × 20 cm) oven-safe dish. Add a thick layer of the tofu and vegetable mixture overtop, then top with the rest of the eggplant. Finish with the bechamel sauce, smoothing it down with the back of a wooden spoon.

Bake for 40 minutes in the preheated oven, switching to a broil for the last 5 minutes to get a bit of a golden-brown colour on the top.

Remove from the oven and let it rest for 10 minutes before serving. Bon appetit!

BECHAMEL

4 cups (1 L) soy milk

1 clove garlic, smashed

1 bay leaf

1 shallot, sliced

1 pinch nutmeg

½ cup (125 mL) olive oil

⅔ cup (160 mL) all-purpose flour

Kosher salt

Fresh black pepper

CHIVE GNOCCHI *with* WILD MUSHROOMS FLORENTINE

MAKES 4–6 SERVINGS

3 lb (1.3 kg) russet potatoes, pricked with a fork

2½ cups (625 mL) all-purpose flour + more as needed

½ Tbsp (7 mL) kosher salt

¼ cup (60 mL) finely chopped chives

1 tsp (5 mL) aged balsamic vinegar, for serving

¼ cup (60 mL) grated vegan Parmesan, for serving

MUSHROOM FLORENTINE SAUCE

1 Tbsp (15 mL) olive oil

2½ cups (625 mL) oyster mushrooms, broken up into pieces

2½ cups (625 mL) king oysters, cut in half then sliced into ¼-inch (0.5 cm) thick slices

2½ cups (625 mL) maitake mushrooms, broken up into pieces

3 cloves garlic, minced

Kosher salt

3 Tbsp (45 mL) corn starch

1 cup (250 mL) soy milk

1 cup (250 mL) vegetable stock (for homemade, see page 114)

2 Tbsp (30 mL) nutritional yeast

1 tsp (5 mL) lemon juice

2 cups (500 mL) spinach leaves

Fresh black pepper

Gnocchi are light pillows of pasta begging for a rich and flavourful sauce. This soy-based, umami-centric mushroom sauce coats each and every gnocchi, creating a hearty dish that is perfect to share with family and friends.

Preheat oven to 185°C (375°F).

Bake the potatoes directly on the oven rack for 50–75 minutes, or until soft and tender, then remove from the oven and allow them to cool.

Peel the skins off the potatoes and rice them (it's best to put them through a tamis to avoid lumps). Place the potato pulp in a medium bowl and add the flour little by little while stirring. Knead the mixture until all the flour is incorporated and the dough is no longer sticky. Add the salt and, if the dough is still sticky, add up to another ½ cup (125 mL) flour. Continue to knead until you have a smooth ball of dough.

Bring a large pot of salted water to a boil. On a lightly floured bench, roll the dough into long thin ropes. Cut the ropes into 1-inch (2.5 cm) squares and roll them across the tines of a fork to leave an impression. Add about 10–15 gnocchi at a time to the boiling water (so that the water doesn't drop too much in temperature) and boil until they float. Remove the gnocchi with a slotted spoon and place them in a medium bowl. Repeat until all the gnocchi are cooked.

MUSHROOM FLORENTINE SAUCE Heat the olive oil in a large skillet over medium-high heat. Add all of the mushrooms and sauté until golden brown (don't stir too much). Add the garlic and 1 tsp (5 mL) salt.

In a medium bowl, mix the corn starch, soy milk and vegetable stock together and whisk until fully combined. Add the corn starch mixture to the mushrooms and reduce heat to medium-low; cook until thickened, stirring occasionally. Add the nutritional yeast and lemon juice and season with salt and pepper to taste.

Add the spinach and stir; cook until the spinach is wilted. Reduce heat to low and adjust the seasoning with salt and pepper if needed.

ASSEMBLY Toss the gnocchi in the mushroom sauce to combine, then add the chives and stir them in. Divide among 4 coupe bowls and serve immediately with a drizzle of balsamic vinegar and a sprinkling of vegan Parmesan shavings.

ZUCCHINI NOODLE PESTO PASTA

MAKES 4–6 SERVINGS

Dig up a taste of Italy right in your own backyard. Lightly cooked zucchini gets dressed up with a bright basil pesto and a squeeze of lemon to create a light summer meal that bursts with flavour. You'll thank me later.

4 zucchinis

Kosher salt

½ cup (125 mL) almond pesto (recipe follows)

1 lemon, juiced and zested

½ cup (125 mL) chopped sun-dried tomatoes

Fresh black pepper

¼ cup (60 mL) grated vegan Parmesan, for serving

8 basil leaves, for garnish

Use a spiralizer to transform the zucchini into noodles, placing them in the machine and cranking the handle until long vegetal noodles are created. Season with 1–2 tsp (5–10 mL) salt and let them sit in a sieve for 10–15 minutes so that they release as much moisture as possible. Pat them dry and set aside.

In a large frying pan, warm 2 Tbsp (30 mL) pesto over medium-low heat and add the noodles. Stir for a minute then add the rest of the pesto with the lemon juice, zest and tomatoes. Season with salt and pepper to taste.

Serve right away in pasta bowls, garnished with shaved vegan Parmesan and fresh basil leaves.

ALMOND PESTO

½ cup (125 mL) raw almonds

8 cups (2 L) fresh basil leaves

3 cloves garlic, smashed

½ cup (125 mL) grated vegan Parmesan

½ cup (125 mL) extra virgin olive oil

Kosher salt

Fresh black pepper

Place the almonds, basil, garlic cloves, Parmesan and one-third of the olive oil in a high-speed blender and blitz until a paste forms. Slowly add the rest of the oil to the blender and season with salt and pepper, if needed.

SAGE *and* BUTTERNUT SQUASH FETTUCINE

MAKES 4–6 SERVINGS

1 recipe vegan pasta dough (recipe follows)

Semolina, for sprinkling on the dough

6 Tbsp (90 mL) extra virgin olive oil + extra for coating the noodles and as needed

2 stalks sage, leaves picked and finely chopped

Sea salt

2 lb (900 g) butternut squash, peeled, seeded and diced small

1 onion, diced

2 cloves garlic, minced

⅛ tsp (0.5 mL) chili flakes

Fresh black pepper

2 cups (500 mL) vegetable stock (for homemade, see page 114)

1 lemon, juiced

¼ cup (60 mL) pine nuts, toasted

This fettucine is oh-so-creamy and oh-so-sweet! With its vibrant orange colour and rich, comforting sauce, this is sure to be your new favourite meatless-Monday family meal!

Cut the dough into 4 equal pieces. Flatten each with a rolling pin and either run through a pasta sheeter or roll by hand until thin (aim for 1/16–⅛ inch/1.5–3 mm thickness). Cut into strips that are 16 inches (40 cm) long and ¼ inch (0.5 cm) wide and sprinkle with a bit of semolina so they don't stick together.

Bring a large pot of salted water to a boil and cook the pasta for no more than 1–2 minutes; drain, but reserve some of the cooking water. Coat the noodles with a bit of olive oil and set aside.

Heat 6 Tbsp (90 mL) olive oil in a large skillet over medium heat. Once simmering, add the sage and toss to coat. Let the sage get crispy, then use a slotted spoon to transfer to a small bowl lined with paper towels. Season lightly with a pinch of salt.

Keep the skillet warm and add the squash, onion, garlic and chili flakes (you can add a little bit more oil if you feel the need). Season with ½ Tbsp (7 mL) salt and ¼ tsp (1 mL) black pepper and cook over medium-low heat for about 10 minutes, stirring occasionally, until the onion is translucent. Add the stock and bring to simmer, then reduce by half.

Make sure the squash is soft before transferring the mixture to a high-speed blender; purée until smooth. Check the seasoning and add salt and pepper if necessary.

Take the same skillet you used for the squash and add the pasta, squash purée and ¼ cup (60 mL) of the pasta cooking liquid; stir to combine. Cook over medium heat, tossing and adding more pasta water as necessary, until the sauce coats the pasta. Check the seasoning and add salt and pepper if necessary, as well as the lemon juice and pine nuts.

Roll the pasta around a long fork or large tweezers until it creates a nest. Place the nest in the centre of each pasta bowl. Top with black pepper, olive oil and fried sage.

VEGAN PASTA DOUGH

In the bowl of a stand mixer fitted with the dough hook attachment, combine the flours and start blending on medium speed. Slowly pour in the hot water and mix until the dough forms into a ball.

Remove the dough and knead it by hand for about 6–8 minutes. Cover the dough in plastic wrap and let it rest in the fridge for at least 30 minutes before rolling out and cutting into pasta.

2 cups (500 mL) semolina flour

1 cup (250 mL) 00 flour

1 cup (250 mL) hot water

MARGHERITA PIZZA

MAKES 1 LARGE OR 2 SMALL PIZZAS

Enjoy a cheesy, hearty, comforting slice of a classic margherita pizza—with no dairy required! All you need are a few cashews and a dash of spice to make this creamy, plant-based rustic pie. Serve with a Kale Caesar (page 92) for a complete meal.

1 recipe vegan pizza dough (recipe follows)

SAN MARZANO PIZZA SAUCE

- ¾ cup (185 mL) crushed San Marzano tomatoes (pulsed with an immersion blender)
- 1 tsp (5 mL) extra virgin olive oil
- 1 clove garlic, minced
- 1 stalk rosemary, leaves picked and chopped
- ⅛ tsp (0.5 mL) onion powder
- 1 tsp (5 mL) kosher salt + more as needed
- ¼ tsp (1 mL) fresh black pepper + more as needed

CASHEW CREAM

- ½ cup (125 mL) raw unsalted cashews
- 1 cup (250 mL) water
- 2 tsp (10 mL) extra virgin olive oil
- 1 tsp (5 mL) rice flour
- ½ tsp (2 mL) garlic powder
- ½ tsp (2 mL) kosher salt
- 1 tsp (5 mL) lemon juice
- ¼ tsp (1 mL) onion powder
- ½ tsp (2 mL) miso

GARNISHES

- 6 basil leaves
- 1 lemon, zested
- Cracked black pepper
- Chili oil (page 67), for serving

Prepare the pizza dough as directed, then place it in a bowl covered with plastic wrap. Let it proof (for the second time) in a warm environment for 90–120 minutes.

SAN MARZANO PIZZA SAUCE In a medium bowl, pulse the tomatoes with an immersion blender until they start to break down (or you can chop them up). Add all the remaining San Marzano pizza sauce ingredients and stir to combine; adjust the seasoning with more salt and pepper, if necessary.

CASHEW CREAM Fill a bowl with hot water and soak the cashews for 15 minutes, then drain. Add the cashews to a high-speed blender with the remaining cashew cream ingredients. Blend until completely smooth.

Add the cashew cream to a skillet over medium heat and cook until evenly thickened, about 5 minutes. Stir occasionally to avoid sticking to the bottom and burning. Adjust the seasoning with salt and set aside.

ASSEMBLY Preheat oven to its highest setting, ideally 260–315°C (500–600°F).

Flour the counter and form the dough into a ball; flatten and spread it out using your hands. Keep spreading to make 1 large pizza or 2 small. (Make sure the dough is thin, as it will rise while baking.)

Place the dough on a parchment-lined baking sheet. Using a ladle, add the pizza sauce on top and spread it evenly across the dough using the back of the ladle; add some cashew cream and basil leaves overtop.

Bake for about 8–12 minutes (the exact time will depend on the oven temperature); the dough should be puffed and achieve a nice golden-brown colour. Remove from the oven and add some lemon zest and fresh pepper on top. Slice and serve with chili oil on the side. Buon appetito!

VEGAN PIZZA DOUGH

½ cup + 1 Tbsp (140 mL) warm water (about 45°C/100°F)

1 tsp (5 mL) dry active yeast

1¼ cups (310 mL) 00 flour, divided

⅓ tsp (1.5 mL) kosher salt

1 Tbsp (15 mL) semolina flour

2 tsp (10 mL) extra virgin olive oil

In a small bowl, combine the warm water with the yeast and 1 Tbsp (15 mL) 00 flour. Mix well with a fork or whisk and cover the bowl with plastic wrap; let sit for 10 minutes.

In the bowl of a stand mixer fitted with the dough hook attachment, mix together the salt, semolina, olive oil and remaining 00 flour on low speed. Add the water–yeast mixture and mix well on medium speed until the dough is smooth, about 10 minutes. Let it sit for 5 minutes.

Place the dough on the counter and knead it until completely smooth. Put it in a new bowl and cover with a hot, wet towel; let the dough rise for 30 minutes.

Once proofed you can wrap the dough in plastic or place it in a vacuum seal bag and freeze it, or you can wrap it and keep it in the fridge for 2–3 days.

NOTE: If you don't have a mixer, you can knead it by hand.

2.5KG

Chef Felicia De Rose

DESSERTS, PASTRIES *and* CONFECTIONS

PECAN AND PAIN D'ÉPICES ECLAIRS

MAKES 10–12 ECLAIRS

Choux pastry dough (or pâte à choux) is the piping dough used for items such as profiteroles, éclairs, gougères and others. The original round piped cream puffs resembled cabbages ("choux" in French) and were named for this likeness. This modern take on the éclair comes fully loaded with your favourite fall spices.

Preparing choux is a great skill to learn, but it requires a baker's hand. It might not be the first recipe to try if you're a beginner; however, the second you nail this recipe, a whole new world of pastry will open up to you.

1 batch choux pastry dough (recipe follows)

CRAQUELIN

½ cup (125 mL) unsalted vegan butter

½ cup (125 mL) sugar

¾ cup (185 mL) all-purpose flour

1 tsp (5 mL) ground cinnamon

½ tsp (2 mL) ground nutmeg

½ tsp (2 mL) ground cloves

½ tsp (2 mL) ground ginger

¼ tsp (1 mL) ground cardamom

CANDIED GINGER

One 4-inch (10 cm) piece fresh ginger, skin scraped off

¼ cup (60 mL) sugar + extra for coating

½ cup (125 mL) water

... ingredients continued

Prepare the choux pastry dough. Wrap in plastic and set aside in the fridge.

CRAQUELIN Combine all the craquelin ingredients in the bowl of a stand mixer fitted with the paddle attachment and mix on medium speed until just combined. Remove the dough and roll between 2 pieces of parchment paper with a rolling pin until about 1⁄16 inch (1.5 mm) thick. Carefully cut into 6- × 1-inch (15 × 2.5 cm) rectangles and place them on a parchment-lined baking tray. Cover the tray with plastic wrap and freeze until ready to use.

CANDIED GINGER Slice the ginger into 1⁄16- to ⅛-inch (1.5–3 mm) thick pieces and place in a small pot, top with cold water and bring to a boil. Once boiling, strain and refresh the ginger in a bowl of ice water. Repeat the process 3 times.

In a small pot, bring the sugar and water to a boil and add in the blanched ginger. Cook everything to 107°C (225°F) then strain the syrup through a sieve and carefully toss the syrup-coated ginger in extra sugar to coat it. Transfer the sugared ginger to a cooling rack and let it rest at room temperature for 4 hours, or until dry.

Once dried, julienne the ginger into small matchsticks.

... recipe continued

CANDIED PECANS

¼ cup (60 mL) sugar

¼ cup (60 mL) water

½ cup (125 mL) pecans, lightly toasted

PECAN PRALINE PASTE

1 cup (250 mL) pecans

½ cup (125 mL) blanched almonds

¼ cup (60 mL) maple syrup

½ cup (125 mL) brown sugar

½ vanilla bean, scraped

PAIN D'ÉPICES CREAM

One 14 oz (400 mL) can coconut milk (full fat), refrigerated for at least 12 hours

1 tsp (5 mL) vanilla paste (or ½ tsp/2 mL vanilla extract)

1½ Tbsp (22 mL) maple syrup

1 tsp (5 mL) ground cinnamon

½ tsp (2 mL) ground nutmeg

½ tsp (2 mL) ground cloves

½ tsp (2 mL) ground ginger

¼ tsp (1 mL) ground cardamom

CANDIED PECANS In a small saucepan, heat the sugar and water to 110°C (230°C). Toss the lightly toasted nuts into the pot, making sure the nuts are still warm so as to not shock the temperature of the sugar syrup. Using a wooden spoon, vigorously stir the nuts to evenly coat them in the sugar, which will begin to stick to the nuts and crystallize. Continue cooking and stirring the nuts over medium-low heat until the sugar crystals start to caramelize and turn a golden amber. Remove from heat and pour the nuts onto a parchment-lined baking tray.

Wearing heatproof gloves, spray your hands lightly with cooking spray and separate the nuts on the tray, making sure they are not touching one another. Set aside to cool.

PECAN PRALINE PASTE Heat oven to 170°C (340°C) and roast the nuts on a parchment-lined baking tray for 10–12 minutes, until they become a toasty golden brown and their oils begin to release.

In a medium pot, heat the maple syrup, sugar and vanilla bean over medium heat; stir, but only until the sugar dissolves. Once the syrup starts to bubble, add in the pecans and almonds. Reduce heat to medium-low and continue cooking for about 6 minutes, stirring continuously, until the sugar syrup reduces and begins to crystallize on the nuts. Continue cooking until the sugar caramelizes, then transfer the nuts to a tray lined with a nonstick baking mat.

Allow the mixture to cool fully before breaking into shards and tossing into a food processor. Blitz on high until a smooth, nutty paste is formed. Cool to room temperature, then cover and set aside.

CHOUX PASTRY Increase oven temperature to 190°C (380°F).

Transfer the choux pastry dough to a piping bag fitted with a medium-sized round tip and begin to pipe the eclairs onto a parchment-lined tray; each should be roughly 6 inches (15 cm) long and ¾ inch (2 cm) wide.

Take the craquelin from the freezer and place 1 precut strip on top of each éclair. Bake for 20 minutes, then drop the temperature to 160°C (325°F) for an additional 15 minutes, or until the choux has browned slightly and dried out.

PAIN D'ÉPICES CREAM Carefully open the can of coconut milk and scoop out the coconut fat into a medium bowl, leaving the liquid behind. Whip the fat into stiff peaks, just as you would whip cream. Add the vanilla paste, maple syrup and all of the spices, then whip for an additional 20 seconds until evenly incorporated. Transfer to a piping bag fitted with a medium-sized star tip.

ASSEMBLY Horizontally slice the top third off of each éclair and set aside. Pipe or drizzle a thin layer of pecan praline paste on the bottom part of the éclairs, then pipe the pain d'épices cream overtop to fill the rest of the choux and add volume. Use the candied pecans and ginger as garnish on top of the cream, then replace the éclair tops.

CHOUX PASTRY DOUGH

- ⅓ cup (80 mL) water
- ⅓ cup (80 mL) soy milk
- ½ tsp (2 mL) kosher salt
- 1 tsp (5 mL) sugar
- 3 Tbsp (45 mL) unsalted vegan butter
- ¾ cup (185 mL) all-purpose flour
- 1 pinch xanthan gum
- Egg replacer equivalent to 3 eggs
- 6 Tbsp (90 mL) aquafaba
- 2 tsp (10 mL) baking powder
- ½ tsp (2 mL) apple cider vinegar

In a medium saucepan, combine the water, soy milk, salt, sugar and butter and warm over medium heat until it reaches a slow simmer. Add in the flour and xanthan gum and, using a wooden spoon, mix vigorously until a wet dough is formed. Continue to stir while cooking for 5–7 minutes, until there are no visible pockets of flour left and the dough begins to dry out, leaving a thin skin on the bottom of the pot.

Transfer the dough to the bowl of a stand mixer fitted with the paddle attachment and mix on medium speed for 4–5 minutes, allowing the dough to cool.

In a medium bowl, prepare the egg replacer according to the instructions on the box. Once thickened, add the aquafaba, baking powder and vinegar and stir to combine until smooth. Slowly add this to the dough and mix on low speed until fully incorporated. Use immediately.

BLACK PLUM BEIGNETS

MAKES 16 BEIGNETS

1¼ tsp (6 mL) potato starch
¼ tsp (1 mL) tapioca starch
½ tsp (2 mL) baking powder
⅛ tsp (0.5 mL) baking soda
½ cup + 2 Tbsp (155 mL) water, divided
1 tsp (5 mL) instant yeast
3½ cups (875 mL) all-purpose flour
½ cup (125 mL) sugar
½ tsp (2 mL) kosher salt
¾ cup (185 mL) vanilla almond milk
3 Tbsp (45 mL) unsalted vegan butter, melted and cooled
Vegetable oil, for frying
¼ cup (60 mL) icing sugar, for garnish
1 lemon, zested, for garnish

PLUM FILLING

7–9 large black plums, pitted, divided
¼ cup (60 mL) water
½ cup (125 mL) sugar
2 Tbsp (30 mL) corn starch
1 cup (250 mL) soy milk
2 Tbsp (30 mL) lemon juice

Just a little taste of New Orleans—because who doesn't love a deep-fried fritter! Bursting with a ripe plum filling, you'll be reaching out for seconds and thirds.

In the bowl of a stand mixer fitted with the dough hook attachment, whisk together the potato starch, tapioca starch, baking powder and baking soda with 2 Tbsp (30 mL) water until smooth and fully combined (this mixture will act as a replacement for eggs). To this, add the yeast, flour, sugar, salt, almond milk and the remaining ½ cup (125 mL) water; mix on low speed for 5 minutes. Add the melted butter and mix for an additional 5 minutes on medium speed until the dough comes together, smooth and soft.

Round up the dough in the bowl and form into a ball. Cover the bowl with plastic wrap and let it sit at room temperature for 1 hour until the dough has doubled in size. Transfer the bowl to the fridge and allow it to rest for another 30 minutes.

PLUM FILLING Roughly chop 5–6 plums and place them in a medium pot with ¼ cup (60 mL) water over medium heat. Cook until the fruit begins to break down, about 5–10 minutes, stirring and adding splashes of water as necessary to prevent the plums from scorching.

Once soft, transfer the cooked plums to a food processor and blend on high until liquefied and smooth. Use a sieve to strain the lumps out of mixture then return to the stove, adding in the sugar, corn starch and soy milk. Cook over medium heat, whisking continuously and vigorously until the mixtures thickens, about 6 minutes. Remove from heat.

Peel and small dice the remaining plums; add the lemon juice and diced plums to the filling mixture (for texture and added freshness). Allow the mixture to cool completely before transferring to a piping bag fitted with a small round piping tip.

DEEP FRYING Lightly flour your work surface and begin to roll out the dough into a large square about ½ inch (1 cm) thick. Use a sharp knife to cut the square into 16 smaller squares roughly 2½ × 2½ inches (6 × 6 cm) each. Space the squares out on a parchment-lined tray and cover gently with plastic wrap. Allow the dough to proof for another 30–45 minutes, or until doubled in size.

Fill a deep, wide frying pan halfway with oil and heat to 175°C (350°F). Fry the beignets 3–4 at a time, frying for about 2 minutes per side or until a nice medium golden brown is achieved. Use a slotted spoon to remove the beignets from the oil, then dry them on a paper towel–lined baking tray.

ASSEMBLY Use a small piping tip to poke a hole in the side of each beignet, gently wiggling while inside to create space for the filling. Insert the tip of the piping bag filled with plum filling into each hole and carefully but generously fill the beignets. Dust the filled beignets with icing sugar and lemon zest.

SUMMER BERRY KOUIGN-AMANN

MAKES 12 KOUIGN-AMANN

4 cups (1 L) bread flour, divided + extra for dusting

½ Tbsp (7 mL) kosher salt

½ Tbsp (7 mL) instant yeast

1 cup (250 mL) water

½ cup (125 mL) oat milk

1¾ Tbsp (28 mL) unsalted vegan butter, divided

¼ cup (60 mL) vegetable shortening + extra for greasing

1 cup (250 mL) sugar + extra for the tart rings

1 cup (250 mL) blueberries

¾ cup (185 mL) tayberries

2 Tbsp (30 mL) icing sugar, for garnish

½ lemon, zested, for garnish

The laminated doughs of layered butter and flour that we all typically love to see in puff pastry or croissants get a new spin when you incorporate a jacket of sugar into those layers, known as kouign-amann. We now get a soft, flaky pastry with a crisp, caramelized exterior, topped with sweet, juicy berries.

Lamination is a lengthy and quite difficult process that requires a couple days to make and is recommended for the advanced baker.

In the bowl of a stand mixer fitted with the dough hook attachment, combine 3¾ cups (935 mL) bread flour with the salt, yeast, water and oat milk. Mix on medium speed for 5 minutes until combined, then add 1½ Tbsp (22 mL) butter. Increase to high speed and continue to mix for another 5 minutes until smooth.

Remove the dough and, using a rolling pin, roll into a 2-inch (5 cm) thick flat square. Wrap the dough in plastic and store in the fridge for 2 hours or overnight.

In the bowl of a stand mixer fitted with the paddle attachment, add the remaining 1¼ tsp (6 mL) butter, the shortening and ¼ cup (60 mL) bread flour and mix on medium speed until smooth. Transfer the mixture to a sheet of parchment paper or plastic wrap and shape into an 8- × 6-inch (20 × 15 cm) block. Store in the fridge for 1 hour, until ready to use.

Take the butter block out of the fridge and let it sit at room temperature for 15 minutes. Take the chilled dough from the fridge and place it on a lightly floured surface; roll it out into a rectangle roughly 8 × 12.5 inches (20 × 31 cm), then place the butter block in the centre. (The dough and the butter should be the same temperature, pliable but on the colder side, to ensure that the butter doesn't melt into the dough; however, the butter shouldn't be so cold that it splits and breaks inside the dough. If at any point during the process the butter/dough feels warm or doesn't roll out easily, allow it to relax and rest in the fridge for 15 minutes before trying again.)

Fold the sides of the dough inwards over the butter like a book to enclose it. Roll this out to roughly 8 × 18 inches (20 × 45 cm). With the dough lengthwise in front of you, grab the left side and fold it over a quarter of the dough. Grab the right side of the dough and fold it over the other three-quarters to meet the edge of the left-side fold. Fold the entire dough once more, this time in half from left to right. The folded dough should now be 8 × 4.5 inches (20 × 11 cm); this is our first "double" fold. Wrap the dough in plastic and let it rest in the fridge for 30–40 minutes.

Remove the dough from the fridge and roll it out again to 8 × 18 inches (20 × 45 cm), repeating the previous double fold technique, except instead of using flour to dust your surface, use 1 cup (250 mL) sugar. As the dough is rolled out, the sugar will incorporate into the dough in a thin layer. Rewrap with plastic and rest for another 30–40 minutes in the fridge.

Remove the dough from the fridge and roll it out one more time into a final sheet that is 16 × 12 inches (40 × 30 cm) in size and about ¼ inch (0.5 cm) thick. Using a pizza cutter or sharp knife, cut this sheet into twelve 4 × 4 inch (10 × 10 cm) squares. Take a square and fold its 4 corners into its centre, applying enough pressure to keep the corners in place. Repeat this with the remaining squares.

Grease twelve 3-inch (8 cm) tart rings (or a 12-cup muffin tin) with vegetable shortening and sprinkle with sugar. Place the rings on a parchment-lined tray and add a kouign-amann to each cavity. Cover the tray with plastic wrap and let it proof at room temperature for about 60–90 minutes, or until the dough has puffed up in size.

Preheat oven to 190°C (380°F).

During the proofing process, the corners should open back up, leaving a cavity in the centre of each pastry. Remove the plastic and place an assortment of berries inside these openings, then bake for 8 minutes. Drop the temperature to 175°C (350°F) and bake for an additional 10–12 minutes, or until the edges are golden brown.

While still hot, carefully remove the tart rings using heatproof gloves or a towel, then allow the kouign-amann to cool on a rack before dusting lightly with icing sugar and fresh lemon zest.

STRAWBERRY MACARONS

CUCUMBER AND LIME GRANITÉ

SUMMER BERRY KOUIGN-AMANN

COCONUT PANNA COTTA

MAKES 6 SERVINGS

½ vanilla bean, scraped
½ lime, zested
3 Tbsp (45 mL) sugar
2½ cups (625 mL) coconut milk
¾ cup (185 mL) coconut cream (full fat)
1½ Tbsp (22 mL) melted cocoa butter
1 tsp (5 mL) agar-agar powder

MERINGUE SHARDS

½ cup (125 mL) aquafaba
¼ cup (60 mL) sugar
⅛ tsp (0.5 mL) cream of tartar
¼ cup (60 mL) desiccated unsweetened coconut

CITRUS ELDERFLOWER GEL

½ cup (125 mL) lemon juice, strained
½ tsp (2 mL) vanilla paste
¾ tsp (4 mL) yellow pectin
¼ cup (60 mL) sugar
2 Tbsp (30 mL) St. Germain elderflower liqueur

COCONUT SNOW

¼ cup (60 mL) coconut oil
3 Tbsp (45 mL) tapioca maltodextrin
2 Tbsp (30 mL) icing sugar

Silicone molds come in all shapes and sizes and are the perfect way to change up the look of boring classics. We've set our panna cotta in a rose silicone mold, to make this all-white plated dessert look anything but bland and to gear us up for the upcoming perennial bloom!

Rub the vanilla bean and lime zest into the sugar and add to a medium pot with the coconut milk and coconut cream; bring to a simmer over medium heat. Once the pot is simmering, slowly whisk in the melted cocoa butter, then add the agar-agar. Allow the mixture to boil for 2 minutes, then strain into 6 silicone molds or 4 oz ramekins. Let it cool while you continue with the recipe.

MERINGUE SHARDS Preheat oven to at 120°C (250°F).

In the bowl of a stand mixer fitted with the whisk attachment, whip the aquafaba on medium speed until it begins to foam. Add the sugar and cream of tartar and continue whipping until stiff peaks form.

Use an offset spatula to evenly spread the meringue over a nonstick baking mat and sprinkle the coconut overtop. Bake for 10–12 minutes, until dry, keeping an eye out to make sure the meringue doesn't brown. Remove from the oven and cool, then break into 2- to 3-inch (5–8 cm) shards and set aside.

CITRUS ELDERFLOWER GEL In a small saucepan over medium heat, bring the lemon juice and vanilla paste to a simmer. In a small bowl, whisk the pectin into the sugar to help prevent clumps and, while whisking, sprinkle the mixture into the vanilla and lemon mixture. Increase heat to high and boil for 2 minutes, then remove from heat and whisk in the elderflower liqueur. Cool completely, then transfer to a small squeeze bottle or piping bag.

COCONUT SNOW In a double boiler over medium-low heat, gently melt the coconut oil, then remove from heat and bring it down to room temperature. In a large bowl, whisk the maltodextrin and sugar together; continue whisking while drizzling in the coconut oil until all the liquid is absorbed and only a powder remains.

ASSEMBLY Scatter coconut snow onto the bases of 6 plates. Gently unmold a panna cotta over each and surround it with shards of meringue. Pipe droplets of citrus elderflower gel over the panna cotta to mimic dew drops and add larger dots around the plate.

CHOCOLAT, CHOCOLAT BROWNIES

MAKES 10–12 BROWNIES

So rich and decadent we named it twice. This chocolate brownie topped with chocolate mousse may look a little fancy but it's super simple, built on a foundation of quality cocoa powder and vegan chocolate.

- 3 cups (750 mL) dark chocolate chips, divided
- 2 Tbsp (30 mL) unsalted vegan butter
- 1¾ cups (435 mL) all-purpose flour
- 2 Tbsp (30 mL) cocoa powder
- 1 tsp (5 mL) baking powder
- 1¾ cups (435 mL) sugar
- ½ cup (125 mL) vegetable oil
- 2 cups (500 mL) vanilla almond milk
- 1 cup (250 mL) walnuts, toasted + extra for garnish (optional)
- ¼ cup (60 mL) roughly chopped chocolate, for garnish (optional)

CHOCOLATE MOUSSE

- 1 cup (250 mL) dark chocolate chips
- 6 Tbsp (90 mL) maple syrup
- ½ cup + 1⅔ Tbsp (150 mL) vanilla almond milk
- ¼ cup (60 mL) cocoa powder
- 3 ripe avocados, pitted and sliced

Preheat oven to 180°C (370°F).

In a double boiler over medium-low heat, gently melt 2 cups (500 mL) dark chocolate chips with the vegan butter, stirring occasionally. Set aside to cool slightly, about 4–5 minutes.

In a large bowl, sift together the flour, cocoa powder and baking powder then whisk in the sugar. Whisk in the oil and almond milk, then fold in the melted chocolate mixture. Add the remaining 1 cup (250 mL) chocolate chips and the nuts (if using). Pour everything into a 9- × 13-inch (23 × 33 cm) parchment-lined tray and bake for about 25 minutes, or until a toothpick inserted into the brownies comes out clean.

Remove from the oven and let the brownies cool in the tray. Once cooled, remove brownies from the tray and cut them to your desired size, typically about 10–12 squares (see note following recipe).

CHOCOLATE MOUSSE In a double boiler over medium-low heat, gently melt the chocolate. Remove from heat and add the maple syrup and almond milk; sift in the cocoa powder, stirring to combine, then cool slightly.

Blitz the avocados in a food processor until smooth, then add the chocolate mixture and process until smooth. Cool in the fridge.

ASSEMBLY Spread or pipe the mousse evenly over the cooled brownies. Garnish with the remaining walnuts and chopped chocolate, if desired.

NOTE: For clean and easy cutting, stick the brownies in the fridge until firm. Heat a knife under hot water then dry it before slicing; repeat this before each slice. Store brownies in a sealed airtight container in the fridge, but let them sit at room temperature for 30 minutes before serving.

BLACK CHERRY CLAFOUTIS

MAKES 8–10 SERVINGS

We're taking this traditional baked French fruit dessert and making it vegan—without compromising the silky flan-like texture of the original. This recipe is simple and requires minimal effort but has maximum payoff. Try substituting cherries with another fruit like berries or plums!

- 1 cup (250 mL) black cherries (fresh or frozen)
- 1 Tbsp (15 mL) sunflower oil + extra for greasing
- 12 oz (340 g) block firm silken tofu
- 1 cup (250 mL) all-purpose flour
- 1 Tbsp (15 mL) corn starch
- ¼ cup (60 mL) sugar
- 1 pinch kosher salt
- 6 Tbsp (90 mL) vanilla soy milk
- ½ vanilla bean, scraped
- Icing sugar, for serving

Preheat oven to 200°C (400°F).

If using fresh cherries, pit them and set aside; if using frozen, thaw them completely in a sieve and drain any excess liquid.

In a food processor, blend all the ingredients, except the cherries and icing sugar, on medium speed until smooth.

Grease an iron skillet or baking tray with sunflower oil or any other neutral oil or fat. Pour the mixture into the pan and arrange the cherries evenly on top, pressing them gently into the batter. Bake for about 40 minutes, until set.

Remove from the oven and cool for 20 minutes, then dust with icing sugar. Slice and serve.

TOASTED ALMOND ROCHERS

MAKES 4 SERVINGS

These chocolate-covered nut clusters are sweet, salty and dangerously addictive!

- ¼ cup (60 mL) aquafaba
- 1½ cups (375 mL) slivered almonds
- ¼ cup (60 mL) sugar
- 1 pinch kosher salt
- 1½ cups (375 mL) dark chocolate chips

Preheat oven to 160°C (325°F).

In a medium bowl, whisk the aquafaba for about 3 minutes, until foamy. Toss in the almonds and stir to evenly coat, then add the sugar and salt; stir once more until coated. Spread the mixture onto a parchment-lined baking tray and bake for about 10–12 minutes, or until a toasty brown, giving it a shake halfway through. Remove the tray from the oven and allow the nuts to cool completely before gently breaking up any large clumps.

Melt (or temper, if desired) the chocolate in a double boiler over medium-low heat. Add in the cooled nuts and mix thoroughly to ensure all the nuts are coated. Scoop clusters of the mixture in spoonfuls onto a parchment-lined baking tray to set. Try not to eat them all at once!

RASPBERRY PISTACHIO VACHERIN

MAKES 10 MERINGUES

MERINGUE SHELL

1 cup (250 mL) aquafaba

½ cup (125 mL) sugar

¼ tsp (1 mL) cream of tartar

3 Tbsp (45 mL) chopped pistachios

LEMON CAKE

1 cup (250 mL) all-purpose flour

¾ cup (185 mL) sugar

1 tsp (5 mL) baking soda

¾ tsp (4 mL) kosher salt

¾ cup (185 mL) almond milk

½ cup (125 mL) grapeseed oil

½ Tbsp (7 mL) apple cider vinegar

½ vanilla bean, scraped

1 Tbsp (15 mL) lemon juice

1 Tbsp (15 mL) lemon zest

PISTACHIO SPONGE CAKE

½ cup (125 mL) pistachio paste

½ cup (125 mL) aquafaba

6 Tbsp (90 mL) sugar

¾ cup (185 mL) all-purpose flour

3 N2O cream chargers

In French pastry, vacherin is a dessert vessel made of crisp meringue that is used to hold any filling your sweet tooth desires. Our raspberry pistachio vacherin is an amalgamation of differently textured components that combine for a plated dessert that's sure to impress your dinner guests both in taste and beauty. For a little more pizazz, you can also add candied pistachios and raspberry sorbet and really leave an impression!

MERINGUE SHELL Preheat oven to 120°C (250°F).

Heat the aquafaba in a small pot over medium-high heat until reduced by a quarter, then remove from heat and cool completely. Place the cooled liquid in a mixing bowl and whip with the sugar and cream of tartar until white, fluffy and stiff. Transfer to a piping bag and pipe 10 shells (in the shape of a nest, with a bottom and sides) onto a parchment-lined baking tray: you want to make them about the size of a small fist, and large enough to hold everything in. Sprinkle with chopped pistachios and bake for 12–14 minutes, until nice and crispy. Remove from the oven and cool on the tray while you prepare the rest of the recipe.

LEMON CAKE Increase oven temperature to 180°C (370°F).

Add all the lemon cake ingredients into the bowl of a stand mixer fitted with the whisk attachment and mix until smooth and fully combined. Spread evenly onto a 9- × 13-inch (23 × 33 cm) parchment-lined baking tray and bake for 16–18 minutes or until golden brown.

Remove the cake from the oven and let it cool, then slice into small ½- × ½-inch (1 × 1 cm) cubes. Place the cubes in a medium bowl and cover with plastic wrap; store in the fridge.

PISTACHIO SPONGE CAKE Blend the pistachio paste, aquafaba, sugar and flour in a high-speed blender until smooth. Strain the mixture into a siphon container and charge with 3 N2O chargers; shake well and rest in the fridge for 30 minutes. Fill disposable paper cups (or thick plastic deli containers) halfway with the mixture and microwave for 45 seconds. Let them cool while you continue with the next steps.

RASPBERRY COMPOTE In a small saucepan over medium heat, add the raspberries, water and ⅓ cup (60 mL) sugar and cook down until the natural juices run and the berries begin to break down. Combine the pectin and 6 Tbsp (90 mL) sugar and slowly add to the boiling berries. Simmer gently over medium heat for 2 minutes and add the lemon juice, stirring occasionally. Let the compote cool in a small bowl at room temperature.

VANILLA ALMOND-MILK CREAM In a medium saucepan over medium-high heat, combine all the vanilla almond-milk cream ingredients and boil for 5 minutes or until thick. Allow the mixture to set in the fridge for about 15–20 minutes.

ASSEMBLY Place each meringue shell in the centre of a plate and drop a few pieces of lemon cake inside. Top with a layer of the vanilla almond-milk cream until each meringue is about three-quarters full, then finish to the top with raspberry compote. Garnish with pistachio cake, extra pieces of lemon cake and fresh raspberries.

RASPBERRY COMPOTE

4 cups (1 L) raspberries + extra for garnish

1 Tbsp (15 mL) water

½ cup + 2 Tbsp (150 mL) sugar, divided

4 tsp (20 mL) yellow pectin

2 Tbsp (30 mL) lemon juice

VANILLA ALMOND-MILK CREAM

¼ cup (60 mL) corn starch

½ cup (125 mL) sugar

1 Tbsp (15 mL) vanilla paste

2½ cups (625 mL) vanilla almond milk

BASIL *and* GIN-INFUSED WATERMELON

MAKES 4–6 SERVINGS

- 5 Tbsp (75 mL) gin
- 2 cups (500 mL) fresh basil leaves
- ½ watermelon, rind removed, flesh cut into 1-inch (2.5 cm) squares
- 3 whole lemon peels
- Maldon salt
- 20 basil cress stems and leaves (or small basil leaves)
- Extra virgin olive oil, for serving

Watermelons are 95% water, so why not add a little flavour and fun to all that "empty space"? Rather than serving your guests a watermelon platter, impress them with an elevated version of the popular summertime fruit. This recipe incorporates gin and basil for a unique and refreshing twist that is perfect for any hot day in the sun.

In a medium pot, warm the gin over medium heat. Remove from heat and add the basil leaves; let it infuse as it cools, then pass through a fine mesh sieve.

Place the watermelon in a vacuum seal bag and add the infused gin and lemon peels; seal and leave in the refrigerator for 2 hours. (If you don't have a vacuum sealer, you can use a ziploc bag and infuse for 3–4 hours in the fridge.)

Remove the watermelon cubes from the fridge and place in bowl; sprinkle with salt and basil cress. Add a drizzle of oil and serve right away.

NOTE: You can also put the cubes in the freezer for 20 minutes and serve them semifrozen!

CUCUMBER *and* LIME GRANITÉ

MAKES 10 SERVINGS

- 1 cup (250 mL) sugar
- 1 cup (250 mL) water
- 3 large cucumbers + cucumber slices for garnish
- 5½ Tbsp (82 mL) lime juice + lime wedges for garnish

The perfect palate cleanser to reset your taste buds in between courses, or a refreshing treat to help cool down those hot summer days.

In a small pot, combine the sugar and water and heat to a boil, stirring a couple times. Continue boiling until the sugar dissolves completely, then remove from heat and cool.

Wash and juice the cucumbers in a juicer (or blend in a high-speed blender) and strain, making sure you collect 2½ cups (625 mL) juice. In a shallow container, combine the cooled sugar syrup, cucumber juice, and lime juice and place in the freezer.

Once fully frozen, scrape the mixture into bowls using a fork. Garnish the granité with cucumber slices and lime segments.

TROPICAL FRUIT SALAD *with* GUAVA CREAM

MAKES 4–6 SERVINGS

This is not your average fruit salad cup—it's a tropical-themed combination of natural colours, fresh flavours and pure joy.

VANILLA SYRUP

- 3 Tbsp (45 mL) sugar
- ¼ cup (60 mL) water
- ½ vanilla bean, scraped

GUAVA CREAM

- 1½ cups (375 mL) guava nectar
- ½ cup (125 mL) coconut milk
- 1 pinch xanthan gum
- 2 N2O cream chargers

FRUIT SALAD

- ½ pineapple
- ½ mango
- ½ papaya
- ½ red dragon fruit
- 1 kiwi
- 1 orange
- 12 lychees
- 1 cup + 2 Tbsp (280 mL) hulled strawberries
- 20 grapes
- 10 mint leaves, chiffonaded
- 1 tsp (5 mL) lime juice
- 1 lime, zested

VANILLA SYRUP In a small pot, combine all the vanilla syrup ingredients together and bring to a boil until the sugar dissolves, stirring occasionally. Remove from heat and cool completely.

GUAVA CREAM Blend the guava nectar, coconut milk and xanthan gum together in a high-speed blender. Strain the liquid into a siphon container (you will need a capacity of at least 2 cups/500 mL) and charge with 2 N2O cream chargers. Vigorously shake the canister and let it sit in the fridge for at least 1 hour before use.

ASSEMBLY Peel and slice the pineapple, mango, papaya, dragon fruit and kiwi into bite-sized cubes. Peel and segment the orange. Peel and pit the lychees and slice in half. Cut the strawberries and grapes in half.

Shake the siphon before use and spray out 3 Tbsp (45 mL) guava cream onto 4–6 plates to act as a bed for the fruit salad. In a large bowl, gently toss all the fruit together with the cooled vanilla syrup, lime juice and zest, then playfully arrange it on top of the layer of guava cream.

VANILLA RHUBARB TARTELETTES

MAKES 6 TARTS

What tantalizes the eye more than the vibrant brightness of in-season rhubarb? The beautiful individual-sized tarts you make out of them, of course! These are easy to arrange, pretty to look at and delicious to eat!

VANILLA CREAM

- ½ vanilla bean, scraped
- ¼ cup (60 mL) sugar
- 2 cups (500 mL) vanilla soy milk
- ½ cup (125 mL) all-purpose flour
- 1 Tbsp (15 mL) lemon juice
- ½ lemon, zested

TART SHELL

- 2 cups (500 mL) all-purpose flour
- ½ tsp (2 mL) kosher salt
- 1 tsp (5 mL) sugar
- ¾ cup (185 mL) vegetable shortening, cubed
- ⅓ cup (80 mL) soy milk

. . . ingredients continued

VANILLA CREAM Rub the vanilla into the sugar to evenly distribute, then add to a medium saucepan with all the remaining vanilla cream ingredients, except for the lemon juice and zest. Cook over medium heat for 8 minutes, or until thickened, continuously whisking to ensure the mixture doesn't burn or get lumpy. Remove from heat and whisk in the lemon juice and zest.

Transfer the vanilla cream to a medium bowl and cover with plastic wrap touching the mixture directly (to prevent a skin from forming). Allow it to set in the fridge for 2 hours or until completely cooled.

TART SHELL Preheat oven to 200°C (400°F).

In a large bowl, mix together the flour, salt and sugar. Using a fork or pastry cutter, cut the shortening into the flour until you get a crumbly texture, then slowly add in the soy milk, being careful not to overmix. Add more soy milk, a teaspoon at a time if necessary (if the mix feels too dry), and knead for few minutes until the dough just starts to form a ball.

Dust the counter with a bit of flour and roll out the dough. Cut it into 6 discs large enough to fit into mini tart rings or muffin tins and use the rings to form the discs into tart shells (with bases and sides). Without removing the shells from the rings, let the dough chill for 10 minutes in the freezer.

Remove the shells from the freezer and prick each tart all over with a fork. Remove the shells from the rings (or tins) and place on a parchment-lined baking tray; bake for about 10 minutes, or until the shells begin to turn golden brown. Remove from the oven and cool while you continue the recipe.

. . . recipe continued

RHUBARB COMPOTE

½ vanilla bean, scraped

2 Tbsp (30 mL) sugar

½ lb (225 g) fresh rhubarb, chopped

¼ cup (60 mL) water

VANILLA POACHED RHUBARB

2 stalks fresh rhubarb

½ cup (125 mL) water

¼ cup (60 mL) sugar

½ vanilla bean, scraped

RHUBARB COMPOTE Rub the vanilla scrapings into the sugar to evenly distribute. In a medium pot, toss the rhubarb with the vanilla sugar and water. Cook over medium-high heat, stirring occasionally, until the rhubarb breaks down and becomes soft but retains a bit of bite. Remove from heat and allow to cool completely.

VANILLA POACHED RHUBARB Slice the rhubarb into 1-inch (2.5 cm) thick diagonals and place in a bowl.

In a medium pot, combine the water, sugar and vanilla and bring to a boil; cook until the sugar is fully dissolved, about 4–5 minutes. Pour the hot syrup over the slices of rhubarb and let it sit until the rhubarb has become tender but not mushy. Drain and store the rhubarb on a small baking tray or in a medium bowl, then cover with plastic wrap and place in the fridge until ready to use.

ASSEMBLY Fill each tart shell with vanilla cream, leaving ¼ inch (0.5 cm) at the top to finish off with the rhubarb compote (the filling should be flush with the top of the shell). Arrange the poached rhubarb on top to create a pattern (see image, page 186).

NOTE: The trick to a flaky crust is starting with cold ingredients and cold tools! Stick the bowl, fork/pastry cutter and ingredients in the freezer for 20 minutes before using.

POACHED PEAR CRUMBLE

MAKES 4 POACHED PEARS

The legendary French Chef Auguste Escoffier is credited with creating a dessert named the Poire Belle Hélène, which is made up simply of poached pear and chocolate. We used that as our inspiration for this recipe and added a textured crumble that perfects this super-easy and delicious dessert.

4 ripe but firm pears (Bosc, Bartlett, Anjou)

¼ vanilla bean, scraped

¾ cup (185 mL) sugar

½ cup (125 mL) water

1 cinnamon stick

2 green cardamom pods

2 cloves

One 1-inch (2.5 cm) piece fresh ginger, peeled and sliced

1 cup (250 mL) apple cider

1 cup (250 mL) white wine

Vegan vanilla ice cream, for serving

OAT CRUMBLE

½ cup (125 mL) old-fashioned rolled oats

¼ cup (60 mL) almond flour

¼ cup (60 mL) almond slivers

¼ cup (60 mL) all-purpose flour

¼ cup (60 mL) brown sugar

½ tsp (2 mL) ground cinnamon

¼ tsp (1 mL) ground ginger

1 pinch kosher salt

¼ cup (60 mL) coconut oil

CHOCOLATE SAUCE

¼ cup (60 mL) cocoa powder

¼ cup (60 mL) agave nectar

¼ cup (60 mL) soy milk

1 Tbsp (15 mL) almond butter

½ tsp (2 mL) vanilla paste

Peel the pears, but keep the stems intact. Cut a thin slice off the base of each pear, exposing the core and allowing you to carefully cut/scoop out the seeds.

Rub the scraped vanilla beans into the sugar and place the vanilla sugar and water into a medium pot over high heat; add the cinnamon, cardamom, cloves and ginger. Bring to a boil, stirring occasionally, and cook for about 3 minutes, until the syrup begins to thicken and lightly caramelize. Carefully deglaze with the apple cider and white wine. Once the syrup has fully combined, add the pears to the pot, reduce heat to low and simmer for about 10 minutes, until the pears have softened but still have some structure.

OAT CRUMBLE Preheat oven to 175°C (350°F).

Combine all the oat crumble ingredients in a large bowl and mix with your hands, making sure everything is evenly distributed. Spread evenly onto a parchment-lined baking tray and bake for 15–18 minutes, or until golden brown and crisp. Remove from the oven and let the crumble cool on the tray, then transfer to a medium bowl at room temperature.

CHOCOLATE SAUCE In a double boiler over medium-low heat, combine all the chocolate sauce ingredients and heat for about 3 minutes, whisking until smooth. Keep warm until ready to use.

ASSEMBLY The slice you made off the bottom of the pear should allow it to sit upright on a plate with ease. Sprinkle the oat crumble around each pear and serve them to your guests with a small ramekin of chocolate sauce on the side, so that they can pour as much or little as they wish overtop. Serve with a scoop of vegan vanilla ice cream for the full effect.

STRAWBERRY MACARONS

MAKES 30 MACARONS

MACARON SHELLS

¾ cup (185 mL) aquafaba

1 cup (250 mL) almond flour

1 cup (250 mL) icing sugar

½ vanilla bean, scraped

¼ cup (60 mL) sugar

STRAWBERRY BUTTERCREAM

3 cups (750 mL) hulled and chopped strawberries

1 cup (250 mL) sugar

2 Tbsp (30 mL) light corn syrup

1 cup (250 mL) unsalted vegan butter, diced

1 cup (250 mL) vegetable shortening

STRAWBERRY COMPOTE

3 cups (750 mL) hulled and chopped strawberries

½ cup (125 mL) sugar

2 tsp (10 mL) yellow pectin

1 Tbsp (15 mL) lemon juice

1 lemon, zested

These dainty little French treats with a crispy shell and soft, fruity centre are a labour of love—and completely worth it! This recipe is perfect for adventurous bakers—it's not the most complicated, but it does require a few skills and a bit of time.

MACARON SHELLS In a small pot, add the aquafaba and reduce to ½ cup (125 mL) over medium-high heat. Remove from heat and allow to cool completely.

In a food processor, blend the almond flour and icing sugar together on high speed to get a fine powder; sift into a bowl and set aside.

Rub the vanilla bean into the granulated sugar and evenly distribute.

In the bowl of a stand mixer fitted with the whip attachment, whip the cooled aquafaba with the vanilla sugar on high speed until fluffy and doubled in size. Gently and evenly fold the whipped aquafaba meringue into the flour mixture, then transfer to a piping bag. Pipe small rounds onto a parchment-lined baking tray and tap the tray lightly against the counter, so that any air trapped in the shells is released. Let the piped shells sit at room temperature for about 45 minutes, or until a light skin forms and all rounds are dry to the touch.

Heat oven to 120°C (250°F) and bake the macaron shells for 12–14 minutes. Remove from the oven and cool on the tray while continuing with the recipe.

STRAWBERRY BUTTERCREAM In a small pot, cook the strawberries over medium heat until they start to break down, about 10–12 minutes. Transfer to a high-speed blender and purée until smooth.

Add the blended strawberries to a medium pot with the sugar and corn syrup; cook over medium-high heat until dissolved, about 5 minutes, stirring occasionally. Transfer to the bowl of a stand mixer fitted with the paddle attachment and mix on medium-low speed until the mixture cools to 35°C (95°C). Slowly add the cut-up butter and shortening and continue to mix until combined and smooth. Add the buttercream to a piping bag and set aside.

STRAWBERRY COMPOTE In a small pot, cook the strawberries over medium heat until they start to break down and the liquid from the fruit starts to extract. In a small bowl, thoroughly mix the sugar and pectin together, then sprinkle it into the strawberry mixture while whisking. Boil for 3–5 minutes until the mixture begins to thicken. Remove from heat and stir in the lemon juice and zest.

ASSEMBLY Pipe a small circle of buttercream around the inner rim of a macaron shell, fill its centre with a dollop of strawberry compote and place a second macaron shell on top, sandwiching the filling in between. Repeat with all the remaining shells. If you have any leftovers, macaron shells can be stored in the freezer up to 3 months in a sealed airtight container.

SINGLE-SERVING SPICED PUMPKIN 'PIES'

MAKES 10–12 PIECES

SHORTBREAD

½ vanilla bean, scraped

1 orange, zested

⅔ cup (160 mL) sugar

1¼ cups (310 mL) unsalted vegan butter

2½ cups (625 mL) all-purpose flour

NO-BAKE PUMPKIN FILLING

1¼ cups (310 mL) raw unsalted cashews

Boiling water

1 sugar pie pumpkin

¼ cup (60 mL) coconut cream (full fat)

⅓ cup (80 mL) agave syrup

2 Tbsp (30 mL) coconut oil

1 Tbsp (15 mL) melted cocoa butter

1 tsp (5 mL) vanilla paste

1 Tbsp (15 mL) lemon juice

1 tsp (5 mL) kosher salt

1 Tbsp (15 mL) ground cinnamon

1 tsp (5 mL) ground ginger

½ tsp (2 mL) ground nutmeg

¼ tsp (1 mL) ground cloves

No Thanksgiving is complete without this fall classic to finish the meal. Here's a unique spin on an individual-serving pumpkin pie that will leave a lasting impression on your guests—it elevates the presentation without substituting that same comforting taste. Although quite simple to prepare, it requires a number of steps and some time, so we advise you to review the method carefully before you begin!

SHORTBREAD In the bowl of a stand mixer fitted with the paddle attachment, blend the vanilla and orange zest into the sugar on medium speed, then beat in the butter until combined. Gradually mix in the flour until a dough forms.

With a rolling pin, roll the dough between 2 pieces of parchment paper until you achieve a ⅛-inch (3 mm) thickness. Place the dough on a baking tray lined with parchment paper and rest in the fridge for 1 hour to firm.

Once firmed, portion the rolled out dough into 4½- × 1¼-inch (11.5 × 3 cm) rectangles. Transfer the rectangles back to a parchment-lined tray and return to the fridge for another 30 minutes to allow them to firm once again.

Heat oven to 160°C (325°F) and bake the shortbread dough for 12–14 minutes, or until the edges begin to brown. Remove from the oven, cool and place on a small tray covered with plastic wrap until ready to use.

NO-BAKE PUMPKIN FILLING Place the cashews in a heatproof bowl and pour enough boiling water overtop to completely submerge and cover them. Allow the cashews to sit for at least 1 hour.

Preheat oven to 175°C (350°F).

Slice the pumpkin in half and discard the stem and stringy guts (you can reserve the seeds and roast them for a nice snack!). Place the pumpkin skin-side-up on a parchment-lined tray and roast for 40–50 minutes, or until the flesh can easily be pierced with a knife. Carefully scoop out the flesh and transfer it to a food processor, blending on high speed until smooth. Place the pumpkin on a cheesecloth to drain any excess moisture (this will take about 15–20 minutes).

Drain the cashews and transfer to a food processor. Add ½ cup (125 mL) of the pumpkin purée (cover the rest and store in the fridge) and the remaining no-bake pumpkin filling ingredients and blend on high until smooth. Pour the mixture into a 9- × 13-inch (23 × 33 cm) parchment-lined baking pan with sides (or a baking sheet surrounded by a pastry frame). Smooth the filling, cover with plastic wrap and freeze for 2 hours or overnight.

TORCHED CHAI MERINGUE In the bowl of a stand mixer fitted with the whisk attachment, whip the aquafaba on high speed until foamy, then slowly sprinkle in the sugar and cream of tartar. Continue whipping on high speed until medium peaks form, then add the vanilla extract and spices; continue whipping until the peaks stiffen. Transfer to a piping bag fitted with the tip of your choice (such as a St. Honoré piping tip).

ASSEMBLY Remove the frozen pumpkin filling from the freezer and carefully lift it from the tray. Use a hot kitchen knife to slice it into rectangles that are just slightly smaller on all sides than the shortbread rectangles.

Spread a thin layer of pumpkin purée on top of each shortbread piece to help the filling adhere, then gently transfer a rectangle of filling overtop. Make sure you do this at least 30 minutes before serving so that the shortbread has time to defrost.

Pipe the meringue evenly over the individual 'pies' and use a cooking blowtorch (if available) to gently brown the meringue. Garnish with toasted pepitas, shaved chocolate or any chocolate decorations of your choosing. Serve with your favourite vegan vanilla ice cream on the side!

NOTE: You can freeze any leftover purée in a sealed airtight container up to 3 months.

TORCHED CHAI MERINGUE

½ cup (125 mL) aquafaba

¾ cup (185 mL) sugar

¼ tsp (1 mL) cream of tartar

½ tsp (2 mL) vanilla extract

¾ tsp (4 mL) ground cinnamon

½ tsp (2 mL) ground cardamom

¼ tsp (1 mL) ground ginger

¼ tsp (1 mL) ground nutmeg

⅛ tsp (0.5 mL) ground cloves

GARNISH

¼ cup (60 mL) pepitas, toasted

Chocolate shavings

Vegan vanilla ice cream, for serving

CAKES

TOUCH TO EXPLORE

GALETTE DES ROIS

MAKES ONE 9-INCH (23 CM) CAKE

1 recipe puff pastry (recipe follows)

1 Tbsp (15 mL) maple syrup

1 Tbsp (15 mL) almond milk

1 figurine or almond fève

FRANGIPANE

½ vanilla bean, scraped

½ cup (125 mL) sugar

½ cup (125 mL) unsalted vegan butter

⅓ cup (80 mL) aquafaba

1 cup (250 mL) almond flour

3 Tbsp (45 mL) bread flour

1 Tbsp (15 mL) corn starch

½ tsp (2 mL) baking powder

¼ tsp (1 mL) almond extract

2 Tbsp (30 mL) dark rum

Classic galettes des rois (king's cake) can be found in French bakeries all throughout January to celebrate Epiphany, and are sold with a paper crown. The delicious frangipane filling is baked between discs of puff pastry and contains a single bean (or "fève") hidden somewhere inside. The recipient of the slice that includes the fève gets to bear the crown and become king or queen for the day!

Roll the puff pastry out to a ¼-inch (0.5 cm) thickness. Using a plate or round baking pan to trace, take a sharp knife and cut two 9-inch (23 cm) discs out of the dough.

FRANGIPANE Rub the vanilla bean into the sugar and add to the bowl of a stand mixer fitted with the paddle attachment; add the butter and mix on medium-low speed until smooth, about 8–10 minutes. Add the aquafaba and continue to mix until combined. In a medium bowl, whisk together the almond flour, bread flour, corn starch and baking powder, then slowly add it to the butter mixture and continue mixing until fully combined. Finish with the almond extract and rum and mix until just combined. Cover the bowl with plastic wrap and store in the fridge until ready to use.

ASSEMBLY Preheat oven to 175°C (350°F).

In a small bowl, mix together the maple syrup and almond milk until well combined.

Place one of the puff pastry discs onto a parchment-lined baking sheet. Spread the frangipane over the disc, leaving an inch of space around the edge and making the filling thicker in the centre so that it forms a slight dome. Place the single almond fève anywhere in the filling for the future king/queen to find!

Brush the edges of the disc with some of the maple syrup mixture and place the second disc on top, sealing the sides shut by pressing them down with a fork. Brush the entire top surface with the maple syrup mixture, being careful not to let it drip over the sides of the puff pastry. Seal the layers shut, wrap the tray in plastic and place the tray in the fridge for 30 minutes.

Once rested, use a sharp knife or single razor blade to score a pattern of your choice (be creative) into the top of the galette, then use a knife or fork to pierce a few spots for steam to escape. Bake for about 35 minutes or until golden brown. Remove from the oven, cool slightly and serve.

. . . recipe continued

PUFF PASTRY

3½ cups + ⅓ cup (955 mL) bread flour, divided

1 tsp (5 mL) kosher salt

½ cup + 1 Tbsp (140 mL) cold unsalted vegan butter, divided

1 cup (250 mL) ice water

¼ cup (60 mL) vegetable shortening

In the bowl of a stand mixer fitted with the dough hook attachment, add 3½ cups (875 mL) bread flour and the salt. Cut in ⅓ cup (80 mL) butter and mix on medium speed, slowly adding in the water until the dough combines.

Place the dough on the counter and form into a flat square; wrap in plastic and place in the fridge for 2 hours or overnight.

In a mixer fitted with the paddle attachment, combine the remaining butter, shortening and ⅓ cup (80 mL) bread flour until smooth. Place the mixture on a piece of parchment paper or plastic wrap and shape into an 8- × 6-inch (20 × 15 cm) rectangular block. Place in the fridge, wrapped in plastic, for an hour until ready to use.

Take the chilled dough and, on a lightly floured surface, roll it out to a rectangle roughly 8 × 12½ inches (20 × 31 cm). Take the butter block out of the fridge and let it sit at room temperature for 15 minutes before placing it in the centre of the dough. (The dough and butter should be the same temperature, pliable but on the colder side, to ensure that the butter doesn't melt into the dough, although not so cold that the butter splits and breaks inside the dough. If at any point during the process the butter/dough feels warm, let it rest in the fridge for 15 minutes before trying again.)

Fold the sides of the dough overtop the butter to enclose it like a book. Roll this out to roughly 8 × 18 inches (20 × 45 cm), then fold the dough into thirds, as you would a letter before placing it in an envelope. This is your first fold; the dough should be 8 × 6 inches (20 × 15 cm) once folded. Wrap the dough in plastic again and rest in the fridge for 30–40 minutes.

Remove the dough from the fridge and roll it out again to 8 × 18 inches (20 × 45 cm), repeating the previous envelope fold, then returning back into the fridge wrapped in plastic for another 30–40 minutes. Repeat this step another 4 times, for a total of 6 folds. Allow the puff pastry to rest a final 30–40 minutes before rolling out. If desired, it can be wrapped in plastic and frozen for a later use. It should keep for a couple months.

MULLED WINE ST. HONORÉ

MAKES EIGHT 4-INCH (10 CM) CAKES

This French "cake" was invented in tribute to the French patron saint of bakers and pastry chefs, Saint Honoré. Traditionally a shareable gateau made up of a large disc of puff pastry rimmed with caramel-dipped choux puffs and featuring a crème chiboust in the centre, we transformed this into a glorious personal-sized treat with a modern (and vegan) flare.

1 recipe puff pastry (page 200)

1 recipe choux pastry dough (page 169)

MULLED WINE PASTRY CREAM

1 cup (250 mL) mulled wine (recipe follows)

¾ cup (185 mL) coconut milk (full fat)

½ cup (125 mL) sugar

¼ cup (60 mL) corn starch

1 pinch xanthan gum

MULLED WINE GLAZE

1 cup (250 mL) mulled wine (recipe follows)

½ cup (125 mL) coconut milk (full fat)

1 cup (250 mL) sugar

3 Tbsp (45 mL) light corn syrup

2 Tbsp (30 mL) agar-agar powder

1 pinch xanthan gum

2 Tbsp (30 mL) fresh orange juice

... ingredients continued

Prepare the puff pastry and roll out to a ¼-inch (0.5 cm) thickness. Use ring cutters to cut out eight 4-inch (10 cm) discs and place them on a parchment-lined baking tray; cover the tray with plastic wrap and refrigerate for 30 minutes.

Preheat oven to 175°C (350°F).

Remove the tray from the fridge, discard the plastic and bake for 30 minutes, or until the pastry turns golden brown. Remove from the oven and set aside to cool at room temperature.

Transfer the choux pastry dough to a piping bag fitted with a round tip and pipe four 1-inch (2.5 cm) circles on a parchment-lined tray. Increase oven temperature to 190°C (380°F) and bake for 15 minutes, then drop the temperature to 160°C (325°F) and bake for an additional 15 minutes, or until the choux has lightly browned and dried out. Remove the tray from the oven and set aside to cool at room temperature.

MULLED WINE PASTRY CREAM In a large pot over medium heat, add the mulled wine, coconut milk and sugar and bring to a rolling boil. Mix the corn starch and xanthan gum together and add to the pot, reducing the heat to medium-low and whisking until the mixture has thickened, about 5 minutes.

Transfer the mixture to a bowl and cover with plastic wrap directly touching the surface of the mixture to prevent a skin from forming. Cool in the fridge for 45–60 minutes.

MULLED WINE GLAZE In a medium saucepan over medium-high heat, combine the mulled wine, coconut milk, sugar and corn syrup and heat to 102°C (215°F). Add in the agar-agar and cook at a rolling boil for 1 minute while continuously whisking. Remove from heat and add in the xanthan gum and orange juice, using an immersion blender to blitz until smooth.

... recipe continued

Transfer the glaze into a medium bowl and check the temperature using a candy or digital thermometer: the cream should be applied at 35–40°C (95–105°F).

PIPED COCONUT ORANGE CREAM

- One 14 oz (400 mL) can coconut cream (full fat), refrigerated for at least 12 hours
- ½ tsp (2 mL) orange blossom water
- ½ tsp (2 mL) vanilla paste
- ½ orange, zested

PIPED COCONUT ORANGE CREAM Carefully open the can of coconut cream and scoop out the coconut fat, leaving the liquid in the can. Whip the fat in a bowl until stiff peaks form, just as you would whip cream. Add the orange blossom water and vanilla paste and whip for an additional 20 seconds until incorporated. Fold in the orange zest. Transfer to a piping bag fitted with a medium-sized star tip.

ASSEMBLY Transfer the cooled mulled wine pastry cream to a piping bag fitted with a small round tip and fill the cooled choux puffs by piercing through the bases.

Dip the tops of the filled choux puffs into the mulled wine glaze and allow them to set. Dip the tops of each puff pastry disc in the glaze, shaking off any excess, then place 3 choux puffs evenly spaced on top of one of the discs. Pipe dollops of coconut orange cream in the spaces between the choux and add a rosette in the middle of the disc. Add a final, filled choux on top of the rosette in the centre. Repeat this process to make 8 individual cakes.

MULLED WINE

- 2 cups (500 mL) dry red wine
- ¼ cup (60 mL) brandy
- 1 cinnamon stick
- 2 star anise
- 4 cloves
- 1 orange, sliced

In a large pot over medium heat, combine the wine, brandy, spices and orange and bring to a slight simmer. Continue cooking on low for 15 minutes, then remove from heat and allow the flavours to infuse for an additional 1–2 hours. Strain into a sealed container. Can be stored in the fridge once cooled for about 1 week.

OPERA CAKE

MAKES 10–12 SERVINGS

ALMOND SPONGE CAKE

4 cups (1 L) all-purpose flour

1¼ cups (310 mL) sugar

½ Tbsp (7 mL) baking powder

⅓ cup (80 mL) almond flour

1 cup (250 mL) vegetable oil

2 cups (500 mL) vanilla almond milk

¼ cup (60 mL) dark chocolate chips + ½ cup (125 mL) for garnish

COFFEE SYRUP

1½ cups (375 mL) hot water

1 cup (250 mL) sugar

2 Tbsp (30 mL) instant coffee

1 Tbsp (15 mL) brandy

CHOCOLATE GANACHE

1¼ cups (310 mL) coconut cream (full fat)

1 cup (250 mL) dark chocolate chips or finely chopped chocolate

COFFEE BUTTERCREAM

1 Tbsp (15 mL) instant coffee

1 Tbsp (15 mL) hot water

½ vanilla bean, scraped

¾ cup (185 mL) sugar

1¾ cups (435 mL) aquafaba

½ tsp (2 mL) cream of tartar

1 cup (250 mL) icing sugar, sifted

1¼ cups (310 mL) unsalted vegan butter

1 cup (250 mL) vegetable shortening (high ratio)

. . . ingredients continued

An opera cake is a French staple: a layered cake made of coffee-soaked almond sponge cake, chocolate ganache, coffee buttercream and chocolate glaze. Decadence meets elegance in this beautiful dessert that is always a hit with a crowd!

ALMOND SPONGE CAKE Preheat oven to 175°C (350°F).

In the bowl of a stand mixer fitted with the paddle attachment, add all the almond sponge cake ingredients, except the chocolate chips, and blend on high speed for 5 minutes until smooth. Divide the mixture evenly into 3 portions and pour into three 9- × 13-inch (23 × 33 cm) parchment-lined baking pans. Using a large offset spatula, smooth out the batter as flat and evenly as you can. Bake for 30–40 minutes, then remove from the oven to cool.

COFFEE SYRUP In a medium pot, combine the water and sugar and bring to a boil, stirring occasionally, to create a syrup. Add the instant coffee and whisk to dissolve. Cool completely then add the brandy and stir. Set aside in the fridge.

CHOCOLATE GANACHE In a medium pot, carefully warm the coconut cream over medium-low heat until just simmering, stirring often to ensure the cream does not burn.

Place the chocolate in a heatproof bowl. Pour the hot cream over the chocolate and let it sit for 2 minutes, then gently stir to fully emulsify the ganache without incorporating too many air bubbles. Cool completely, then cover the bowl with plastic wrap and place in the fridge for 1 hour. Before use, remove from the fridge and use a hand mixer to whip to a spreadable consistency.

COFFEE BUTTERCREAM Stir the instant coffee in the water until it dissolves, then set aside.

Rub the vanilla bean into the granulated sugar until evenly dispersed, then add to a medium saucepan with the aquafaba. Bring to a boil for 5 minutes then remove from heat and cool.

. . . recipe continued

CHOCOLATE GLAZE

1 cup (250 mL) semisweet chocolate chips

2 Tbsp (30 mL) vegetable oil

Transfer the aquafaba mixture to the bowl of a stand mixer fitted with the whisk attachment and whip on medium speed until foamy, about 2–3 minutes; add the cream of tartar and increase the speed to high, then add the icing sugar and continue whisking until stiff peaks form. Switch the whisk attachment to the paddle attachment and pour in the coffee mixture. Lower the speed to medium and keep mixing while adding the margarine and shortening; continue until smooth. Cover the bowl with plastic and set aside.

CHOCOLATE GLAZE In a double boiler over medium-low heat, melt the semisweet chocolate chips and stir in the oil until fully emulsified. Check the temperature using a digital thermometer: the glaze should be applied at 40–45°C (105–115°C).

ASSEMBLY In a double boiler over medium-low heat, melt ¼ cup (60 mL) dark chocolate chips. Take one sheet of almond sponge cake and spread a thin layer of melted chocolate on one side, then place on a parchment-lined baking tray and place in the fridge to set, about 20 minutes.

Once set, remove the sponge cake from the fridge and flip it over so the chocolate is on the underside of the cake. Use a brush to thoroughly soak the sheet of sponge cake with a third of the coffee syrup, then, in an even layer, spread half the buttercream overtop using a large offset spatula.

Layer the second sheet of almond sponge cake over the first and soak it with another third of the syrup; spread evenly with half of the chocolate ganache. Add the final sheet of almond sponge cake and soak with the remaining syrup; evenly spread with the remaining buttercream, then the remaining ganache overtop. Finish off with the glaze, pouring it evenly over the top of the cake. In one swift motion, use a large offset spatula to wipe off any excess glaze from the top while preventing it from dripping down the sides.

Melt or temper the remaining dark chocolate to make chocolate decorations of your choosing to ornament the cake with (for example, you could spread the melted chocolate flat, cool it and scrape it with a spatula to create shavings).

CHOCOLATE HAZELNUT BANANA TORTE

MAKES ONE 8-INCH (20 CM) TORTE

Although classified as a cake, a torte has a richer, denser texture and flavour profile, relying less on flour and more on ground nuts. Slathered with chocolate ganache, you're really indulging in decadence with this one! But hey, we threw some bananas in, so . . . that makes it healthy, right?

- 1¼ cups (310 mL) hazelnut flour
- 1⅓ cups (330 mL) all-purpose flour
- ½ Tbsp (7 mL) baking powder
- ½ tsp (2 mL) baking soda
- 1 tsp (5 mL) kosher salt
- 1½ cups (375 mL) mashed fresh bananas (about 4½ medium-to-large bananas), divided + 1 ripe banana
- 1 tsp (5 mL) vanilla extract
- 2 tsp (10 mL) lemon zest
- 1¾ cups (435 mL) aquafaba
- 1⅓ cups (330 mL) sugar, divided
- ½ tsp (2 mL) cream of tartar
- ¼ cup (60 mL) vegetable oil
- 1 cup (250 mL) water
- 1 oz (30 g) Frangelico hazelnut liqueur
- 2 tsp (10 mL) fresh lemon juice
- ¼ cup (60 mL) hazelnuts, toasted, for garnish
- ¼ cup (60 mL) banana chips, for garnish

HAZELNUT PASTRY CREAM

- 2¾ cups (685 mL) almond milk
- ¼ cup (60 mL) sugar
- 5 Tbsp (75 mL) corn starch
- 2 Tbsp (30 mL) melted cocoa butter
- 2 Tbsp (30 mL) hazelnut praline paste (see note)

. . . ingredients continued

Preheat oven to 175°C (350°F). Line four 8-inch (20 cm) round cake pans with parchment paper.

In a large frying pan, gently toast the hazelnut flour over low heat, stirring often, until it turns a soft golden brown. Set aside to cool.

In a large mixing bowl, sift together the all-purpose flour, toasted hazelnut flour, baking powder, baking soda and salt.

In a medium bowl, add ½ cup (125 mL) mashed bananas and stir in the vanilla and lemon zest.

In the bowl of a stand mixer fitted with the whisk attachment, add the aquafaba and whip on medium speed until it becomes foamy. Gently sprinkle in ⅔ cup (160 mL) sugar and the cream of tartar until medium-stiff peaks form.

Scoop a quarter of the aquafaba meringue into the mashed banana mixture and stir to combine. Scoop half the remaining meringue into the bowl of dry ingredients and gently fold the mixture together. Gently add the banana mixture to the batter, continuing to fold. Finally, add the remaining the meringue and fold until just combined.

Divide the batter equally into the 4 pans and bake for about 20–25 minutes, or until springy to the touch and golden brown. Remove from the oven and set aside to cool in the pans.

In a small pot over high heat, combine 1 cup (250 mL) water and the remaining sugar and bring to a boil, stirring occasionally, to create a syrup. Remove from heat and allow to cool completely, then stir in the liqueur. Cover the pot with plastic wrap and place in the fridge.

HAZELNUT PASTRY CREAM In a medium pot, bring the almond milk, sugar and corn starch to a boil. Continue to cook, whisking continuously, for 2–4 minutes, then remove from heat. Stir in the melted cocoa butter and hazelnut paste. Transfer to a bowl and cover with plastic wrap directly touching the surface of the mixture to prevent a skin from forming. Place in the fridge to cool.

. . . recipe continued

CHOCOLATE GANACHE

1¼ cups (310 mL) coconut cream (full fat)

1 cup (250 mL) dark chocolate chips or finely chopped chocolate

CHOCOLATE GANACHE In a medium pot, carefully heat the coconut cream over low heat until just simmering; stir often to ensure it does not burn.

Place the chocolate chips in a heatproof bowl. Pour the hot cream over the chocolate and allow it to sit for 2 minutes before stirring gently (you want to fully emulsify the ganache without incorporating too many air bubbles). Let the ganache cool completely, then cover the bowl with plastic wrap and place in the fridge for 1 hour. Before use, remove from the fridge and use a hand mixer to whip to a spreadable consistency.

BANANA LEATHER Preheat oven to 76°C (170°F).

Peel the ripe banana and purée in a high-speed blender. Spread the banana paste thinly on a silicon baking mat and bake for about 4 hours, or until tacky and easy to peel off the mat. (If you are using a dehydrator, thinly spread the banana on a silicon baking mat and set to 54°C/130°F for 6–8 hours, until you can peel it off easily, then transfer the banana to mesh dehydrator sheets and dry for another 2–4 hours.)

ASSEMBLY Just before building the cake, add the remaining 1 cup (250 mL) bananas to a bowl and mix in the lemon juice.

Place the first layer of cake down on a cake board or stand. Using a brush, soak the layer with the brandy syrup. Spread a layer of hazelnut pastry cream overtop with an offset spatula, followed by an even layer consisting of a third of the bananas and lemon juice.

Add the second layer of cake on top of the first, repeating the process, then repeat again with the third layer. Top with the final layer of cake. Spread the whipped chocolate ganache on the sides of the cake to enclose it. If the icing gets too soft, place it (or the whole cake) back in the fridge to firm, then continue.

Save some ganache and transfer it to a piping bag fitted with a medium-to-large star tip. Pipe rosettes on top of the cake and garnish with banana leather (arranged however you like), toasted hazelnuts and banana chips.

NOTE: If you do not have easy access to hazelnut praline paste or do not want to make your own: Crush and toast ¼ cup (60 mL) hazelnuts, then throw them in a medium pot with the almond milk. Bring to a simmer, remove from heat, cover with a lid and steep for 20 minutes at room temperature. Strain out the hazelnuts and use the infused milk in place of traditional almond milk for the pastry cream, making sure to add more milk for any lost during the cooking process.

APPLE CRANBERRY BABA AU RHUM

MAKES 10 CAKES

2 cups (500 mL) bread flour
1 Tbsp (15 mL) sugar
1 tsp (5 mL) kosher salt
½ tsp (2 mL) instant yeast
¼ cup (60 mL) soy milk
½ cup + 2 Tbsp (155 mL) aquafaba
2 Tbsp (30 mL) melted unsalted vegan butter, cooled
1 Tbsp (15 mL) sunflower oil
1 Granny Smith apple, for garnish
1 Tbsp (15 mL) lemon juice
1 recipe vegan whipped cream (recipe follows), for serving

RUM SYRUP

2 cups (500 mL) water
1 Tbsp (15 mL) vanilla paste (or ½ Tbsp/7 mL vanilla extract)
1 cup (250 mL) sugar
½ cup (125 mL) dark rum

CRANBERRY SYRUP

¾ cup (185 mL) cranberries (fresh or frozen)
1¼ cups (310 mL) apple cider + more as needed
¼ cup (60 mL) sugar
1 tsp (5 mL) vanilla paste (or ½ tsp/2 mL vanilla extract)
¼ cinnamon stick

... ingredients continued

When you take a small little yeast cake and soak it in rum syrup, you end up with a liquor-bloated little dessert known to the French as baba au rhum. We serve it at room temperature, but this drunken treat will be sure to warm you and your winter nights right up!

In the bowl of a stand mixer fitted with the dough hook attachment, add the bread flour, sugar, salt, yeast, soy milk and aquafaba. Mix for 2 minutes on low speed, then for an additional 6 minutes on medium-high until smooth. Return to low speed and begin to drizzle in the melted butter and oil; continue mixing until the dough has fully incorporated the fats. Place in a piping bag.

Pipe the dough evenly into 10 heatproof silicone molds (we recommend savarin molds), filling the molds halfway and leaving room for the dough to rise. Cover with plastic wrap and proof at room temperature for 45 minutes, or until the dough has doubled in size.

Heat oven to 180°C (370°F) and bake the cakes for 18–22 minutes, or until they turn golden brown. Turn the cakes out of the molds onto a cooling rack and cool completely.

RUM SYRUP In a small pot, bring the water, vanilla paste and sugar to a boil until the sugar is fully dissolved, stirring occasionally. Remove from heat and cool for 5–10 minutes before stirring in the rum.

Dip the cakes into the syrup while it's still warm and fully soak them. The cakes should be noticeably plumper and double in size. Set the cakes aside on a wire rack until ready to use.

CRANBERRY SYRUP Place all the cranberry syrup ingredients in a medium saucepan and bring to a boil. Reduce heat to medium-low and simmer for about 10 minutes, until the berries begin to pop and break down. Remove the cinnamon stick and purée the mixture in a high-speed blender until smooth. Thin out with an additional ¼ cup (60 mL) apple cider if necessary. The sauce should be loose and syrupy. Set aside at room temperature.

... recipe continued

CARAMELIZED APPLES

1 Granny Smith apple
1 Golden Delicious apple
1 Honey Crisp apple
2 Tbsp (30 mL) unsalted vegan butter
½ tsp (2 mL) ground cinnamon
¼ tsp (1 mL) ground nutmeg
2 Tbsp (30 mL) brown sugar
1 tsp (5 mL) vanilla paste (or ½ tsp/2 mL vanilla extract)
1 Tbsp (15 mL) Calvados (or brandy)

APPLE GELÉE

1 cup (250 mL) apple cider
4 fresh lemon verbena leaves
1 cup (250 mL) apple juice
2 tsp (10 mL) agar-agar powder
2 Tbsp (30 mL) Calvados (or brandy)

SUGARED CRANBERRIES

¾ cup (185 mL) sugar, divided
½ cup (125 mL) water
½ cup (125 mL) fresh cranberries

CARAMELIZED APPLES Peel and dice all the apples into ½-inch (1 cm) cubes.

In a sauté pan, melt the butter over medium heat. Add the diced apples and cook for 3 minutes, stirring occasionally. Add the spices, sugar and vanilla paste; cook for an additional 3 minutes, stirring occasionally, until the sugar begins to caramelize and the apples become tender but not mushy. Do not overcook the apples, as you want them to hold their shape. Add the Calvados and let the apples simmer in it for 2 minutes before removing from heat. Set aside to cool in a large bowl.

APPLE GELÉE Line an 8- × 8-inch (20 × 20 cm) baking pan with plastic wrap, smoothing it out to get rid of any air bubbles as best as possible.

In a medium pot, add the cider and verbena leaves and bring to a boil. Remove from heat, cover the pot and let the flavour infuse for 40–60 minutes.

After the leaves have steeped, remove them and add the apple juice; bring to a simmer over medium-low heat. Whisk in the agar-agar and continue whisking while the liquid boils for 2 minutes. Remove from heat and allow to cool for 5 minutes before whisking in the Calvados. Pour the mixture into the prepared pan and cover with plastic. Let it set in the fridge for at least 1 hour.

Once set, remove the hardened mixture from the pan and portion it into ½-inch (1 cm) cubes. Keep the cubes in a small bowl covered with plastic wrap in the fridge.

SUGARED CRANBERRIES In a medium pot, bring ½ cup (125 mL) sugar and ½ cup (125 mL) water just to a boil and stir until the sugar has dissolved. Remove from heat and let stand for 5–10 minutes. Add the cranberries and stir just long enough to fully coat each berry in the syrup, then use a slotted spoon to transfer the berries to a wire rack to cool for at least 45 minutes, or until dry but still sticky and tacky. Roll the berries in the remaining sugar to coat and let them dry for another hour.

ASSEMBLY Slice the Granny Smith apple into matchsticks and reserve in cold water with the lemon juice added until ready to use (to prevent browning). Drain the water and pat the apples dry when ready to use.

Ladle a layer of the cranberry syrup into the base of a shallow bowl or a plate with a lip. Place a soaked cake in the centre and place a heaping spoonful of caramelized apples inside the opening. If you used a savarin mold that has a hole in the centre (like a donut), the apples sit nicely inside without creating additional volume, and this grants a flat surface to pipe the whipped cream in any manner you prefer. Finish by garnishing with the cubed gelée, sugared cranberries and fresh apple slices. Repeat with the remaining cakes.

VEGAN WHIPPED CREAM

1 cup (250 mL) raw unsalted cashews

Boiling water, to cover

1 cup (250 mL) water

½ vanilla bean, scraped

½ tsp (2 mL) lemon zest

1 Tbsp (15 mL) sugar

½ cup + 1 Tbsp (140 mL) coconut oil

½ cup + 1 Tbsp (140 mL) unsalted vegan butter

⅔ cup (160 mL) icing sugar

Place the nuts in a heatproof bowl and cover with boiling water; let sit for at least 1 hour to soften.

Drain the water and transfer the nuts to a high-speed blender, adding 1 cup (250 mL) fresh water; blend until smooth.

Rub the vanilla bean and zest into the sugar and place in a medium pot along with the coconut oil and the cashew mix. Cook over medium heat until thick, about 8 minutes, stirring frequently to ensure the mixture doesn't burn. Transfer to a bowl, cover with plastic wrap and place in the fridge for 8 hours or overnight.

In a large bowl, beat together the butter and icing sugar until smooth, then add in the thick, rested cashew mix. Continue beating until stiff peaks form. Reserve in the fridge until ready to use. Keeps for a few days.

MEYER LEMON CHIFFON CAKE

MAKES ONE 9-INCH (23 CM) CAKE

A slice of this vibrant, pillowy cake could help brighten even the darkest of days, and it makes the perfect travel cake to bring to any potluck. We use Meyer lemons for their sweeter, brighter fragrance and depth of flavour, but any lemon will do!

- Vegan butter, for greasing
- 3 cups (750 mL) cake flour + extra for the pan
- 3 Tbsp (45 mL) potato starch
- 1 tsp (5 mL) kosher salt
- 2 tsp (10 mL) baking powder
- ¼ tsp (1 mL) turmeric powder
- 1 vanilla bean, scraped
- 3½ Tbsp (52 mL) lemon zest + extra for garnish
- 1½ cups (375 mL) sugar
- ¼ cup (60 mL) fresh lemon juice
- ½ cup (125 mL) vegetable oil
- 2 Tbsp (30 mL) unsweetened apple sauce
- 1½ cups (375 mL) soy milk
- 5 Tbsp (75 mL) aquafaba
- ¼ tsp (1 mL) cream of tartar
- 1 recipe candied lemon slices (recipe follows), for garnish

LEMON SYRUP

- ¼ cup (60 mL) sugar
- ½ cup (125 mL) water
- 2 Tbsp (30 mL) fresh lemon juice

LEMON ICING

- 1 cup (125 mL) icing sugar + more as needed
- 1 Tbsp (15 mL) water
- 1 Tbsp (15 mL) fresh lemon juice
- ⅛ tsp (0.5 mL) ground green cardamom (optional)

Preheat oven to 175°C (350°F). Grease a 9-inch (23 cm) Bundt or chiffon cake pan with vegan butter and lightly flour.

Sift the cake flour into a large bowl, then whisk in the starch, salt, baking powder and turmeric. Rub the scraped vanilla bean and lemon zest into the granulated sugar and add it to the dry ingredients.

In a medium bowl, mix together the lemon juice, vegetable oil, apple sauce and soy milk; carefully incorporate these wet ingredients into the dry, gently mixing to combine.

In a small bowl, whip the aquafaba and cream of tartar together until soft to medium-stiff peaks form. Gently fold this into the batter. Pour the batter into the prepared pan and bake for 40–45 minutes, or until a toothpick inserted comes out clean.

Remove the cake from the oven and allow it to sit in the pan for 5 minutes before turning out onto a cooling rack.

LEMON SYRUP In a small pot, combine all the lemon syrup ingredients and bring to a boil for 2 minutes. Remove from heat and cool, but apply to the cake while still warm. Brush the syrup all over the still-warm cake to help keep it moist.

LEMON ICING In a medium bowl, whisk all the lemon icing ingredients together until smooth, adding more sugar if necessary until you reach a thick, glossy consistency. Drizzle the icing over the top of the warm syrup-soaked cake and gently tap the cooling rack beneath it so that some of the icing drips down the sides of the cake.

ASSEMBLY Garnish the finished cake with candied lemon slices and fresh lemon zest in whatever pattern you prefer.

CANDIED LEMON SLICES

- 1 lemon, sliced into thin rounds
- ½ cup (125 mL) sugar
- ½ cup (125 mL) water

In a small pot, add the lemon rounds and cover with cold water. Bring to a boil over medium-high heat; once boiling, strain and refresh in a bowl of ice water. Repeat the process 3 times.

In a wide-bottomed pot over high heat, bring the sugar and water to a boil, stirring occasionally. Add the blanched lemon slices, reduce heat to low and cook for 25–30 minutes, until the rinds become translucent. Transfer the slices to a cooling rack and allow them to sit at room temperature for 8 hours or overnight.

Roxanne West

VEGAN BRIDGE MENUS

As we are not just cookbook authors but also chefs, there are few things we do better than arranging a menu for a special occasion. Below are a selection of themed meals—from appetizers to desserts—to inspire you the next time it's your turn to host.

SPRING GATHERING

As the spring harvest begins to pop up from the ground, all the green beauty mother nature has to offer can be gathered into the perfect seasonal meal.

Grissini

Asparagus and Puffed Amaranth (page 70)

or

Fresh Thai Vegetable Roll (page 62)

Zucchini Noodle Pesto Pasta (page 157)

or

Fried Tofu with Sweet Chili Sauce (page 144)

Vanilla Rhubarb Tartelettes (page 187)

or

Meyer Lemon Chiffon Cake (page 214)

HARVEST CELEBRATION

The leaves are falling, the weather is starting to change and you want to get cozy. Welcome to the season of root vegetables and pumpkin spice—two highlights of this homey meal that's perfect for an autumn get-together!

Soft and Chewy Pretzels (page 49)

Roasted Beet Salad with Sherry Dressing (page 103)

or

Coconut Ginger Squash Soup (page 121)

Chive Gnocchi with Wild Mushrooms Florentine (page 154)

or

Sweet Potato Gratin (page 141)

Pecan and Pain d'Épices Eclairs (page 167)

or

Single-Serving Spiced Pumpkin "Pies" (page 192)

VEGAN TAPAS NIGHT

Looking for a one-night vacation? This menu is exactly what you need. It will transport your taste buds to new horizons for an exquisite meal with heavy accents from Central and South America that encourage bold and fresh flavours (with a hint of spice).

Corn Tortillas (page 48)

Coconut "Ceviche" with Pickled Kiwi (page 73)

or

Avocado Fries (page 59) and Tahini Dip (page 36)

Sweet Corn and Tomato Chili (page 126) with Pebre (page 39)

or

Deep-Fried Tomatillo Tacos (page 142)

Tropical Fruit Salad with Guava Cream (page 185)

or

Cucumber Lime Granité (page 184)

SUMMER PICNIC

Brush off your favourite picnic basket and fill it with these delicious dishes. Spread a blanket or towel out on the ground and prepare to eat your heart out while getting your suntan on.

Garlic and Herb Focaccia (page 46)

Cantaloupe and Basil Two Ways (page 55)

or

Summer Heirloom Tomato Salad with Crunchy Quinoa (page 91)

Cobb Salad (page 106)

or

Margherita Pizza (page 160)

Summer Berry Kouign-Amann (page 172)

or

Black Cherry Clafoutis (page 181)

MIDDLE EASTERN FEAST

This collection of recipes will let you experience the magic effect of spices from the Middle East. Warm and spicy flavours envelop you for an incredible culinary adventure.

Poppy Seed and Sesame Lavash (page 51)

Roasted Red Pepper Hummus (page 37) and Baba Ganoush (page 33) with Pita Bread (page 47)

or

Citrus and Lentil Salad (page 99)

Chickpea Power Salad with Green Goddess Dressing (page 96)

or

Green Falafel (page 135) with Tahini Dip (page 36)

Mango Mania Twist Smoothie (page 81)

or

Raspberry Pistachio Vacherin (page 182)

PARISIAN AFFAIR

Who better to trust with this menu than a Paris-born chef? This menu will make you want to put on a beret, grow a mustache and go for a bike ride around town.

Classic Parisian Baguettes (page 44)

Crispy Meunière-Style Cauliflower (page 68)

or

Vegan Vichyssoise (page 117)

Ratatouille-Stuffed Mushrooms (page 132)

or

Cannellini Bean Pot Pie (page 130)

Strawberry Macarons (page 190)

or

Opera Cake (page 204)

WINTER WONDERLAND

Winter is coming, snow is at the door and you need hot dishes to warm your body and soul. These recipes are going to keep your morale high with their bold and hearty flavours until spring has sprung.

Everything and the Bagel (page 50)

Charred Brussels Sprouts (page 71)

or

Cumin and Carrot Soup (page 122)

Lentil Cabbage Rolls in Roasted Tomato Sauce (page 64)

or

Cauliflower Tikka Masala (page 133)

Mulled Wine St. Honoré (page 201)

or

Galette des Rois (page 198)

Irene Matys
FOOD STYLIST

ACKNOWLEDGMENTS

To my parents, thank you for supporting me in my decision to become a chef, but more importantly, thank you for raising me well so I could become the man that I am. Thank you to my brother and family for being there for me and understanding me leaving our country to travel far away and establish a new home away from home.

To my loved one, thank you for believing in me and never doubting me, for keeping me in check and for helping me achieve my dreams. To my friends, thank you for being awesome, lending me an ear to vent and allowing me to be myself, and for making me laugh when times were tough.

Thank you to our amazing photographer, Igor Aldomar, and our stylist, Irene Matys, for making our dishes shine through your lens, vision and talent.

Thank you Alisha Sood for being a fantastic assistant on the shoot, and Kenzie Osborne for assisting with some of the backend of the manuscript.

Thank you to our agent, Chris Casuccio, for believing *The Vegan Bridge* had legs, and to our publisher Whitecap for making it walk.

Thank you to all of our partners, sponsors and suppliers: Bob Park and Monogram Canada, for providing us with a beautiful space to shoot; Jonathan Kim at Phil's Produce, who supplied us with the best fruits and vegetables; and Brae Mason at Mason Epicure, for outfitting our dishes with the most beautiful glass- and plateware.

Thank you to all my vegan chefs and friends for their guest-star appearances. Felicia, Roxanne, Elia, Matthew, I'm glad you were part of the journey. Thank you Chef Matthew Kenney, for writing the first words to the cookbook.

And thank you to our readers, without whom this cookbook would have remained a kitchen-counter journal.

I also want to thank myself for believing in myself—if I didn't, how could I expect you to?

Last but not least, a very special thank you to my co-author and best friend whom I constantly drag into my projects and who never says no. You already know how I feel about you, but thank you for bringing your touch, vision and talent to this book. It wouldn't have been the same without you. I am so happy you agreed to go on this fun adventure with me.

I would like to dedicate this book to the memory of my late grandparents, godfather and young aunt. I wish you could have seen what I've accomplished, but I know that wherever you are, you're proud of me.

–Romain

Alongside all the phenomenal people Romain mentioned who made this book possible, I would just like to dedicate my efforts towards this project and all efforts I make in life to my grandparents and family. Everything I hold sacred in this life revolves around the upbringing they fought to provide for their kin, and I am determined to show them that all their sacrifices, unconditional love and support for me will forever be appreciated.

I'd also like to acknowledge all the chefs out there and the hospitality industry in general. We break our backs both figuratively and quite literally trying to feed peoples' hunger and souls, with art in the form of sustenance, leaving a little bit of ourselves in every creation we send out on a plate. You are the real MVPs.

Lastly, thank you to my partner in crime, my best friend and the one who pulls me kicking and screaming into every project he gets himself into. Work never seems like work when it's with you.

—Richelle

INDEX

D

E

F

R

S